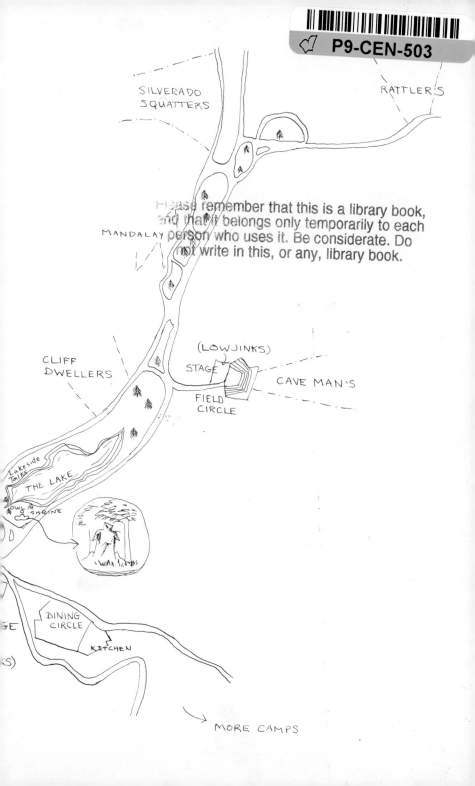

SILVERADO
SQUATTERS

RATTLER'S

MANDALAY

CLIFF
DWELLERS

(LOWJINKS)

STAGE

CAVE MAN'S

FIELD
CIRCLE

Lakeside
Talks

THE LAKE

OWL
SHRINE

DINING
CIRCLE

GE

KITCHEN

S)

→ MORE CAMPS

The Bohemian Grove
and Other Retreats

Books by G. William Domhoff

Fat Cats and Democrats (1972)

The Higher Circles (1970)

Who Rules America? (1967)

C. Wright Mills and The Power Elite
(coeditor with Hoyt B. Ballard, 1968)

WEAVING SPIDERS COME NOT HERE

The Bohemian Grove and Other Retreats

A Study in Ruling-Class Cohesiveness

by G. William Domhoff

HARPER & ROW, PUBLISHERS

New York, Evanston, San Francisco, London

FIRST EDITION

Designed by Janice Stern

Library of Congress Cataloging in Publication Data

Domhoff, G. William.
The bohemian grove and other retreats.
  Includes bibliographical references.
  1. Bohemian Club, San Francisco. 2. Upper classes—United States. 3. Elite
(Social sciences) I. Title.
HS2725.S4B774   367'.973   73–14253
ISBN 0–06–011048–1

To Lynne, Lori, Bill, and Joel

Contents

Preface

In America, retreats are held by just about every group you can think of—scouts, ministers, students, athletes, musicians, and even cheerleaders. So it is not surprising that members of the social upper class would also have clubs that sponsor such occasions. Three of these retreats for the wealthy few are the subject of this book.

Retreats are interesting in and of themselves. They are especially interesting when—like the bacchanalian rites discussed in this book—they involve elaborate rituals, first-class entertainment, a little illicit sex, and some of the richest and most powerful men in the country.

However, this book has a purpose beyond presenting a relatively detailed description of three upper-class watering holes that are of intrinsic interest. Upper-class retreats are also of sociological relevance, for they increase the social cohesiveness of America's rulers and provide private settings in which business and political problems can be discussed informally and off the record. Moreover, their existence is evidence for a theory heatedly disputed by most social scientists and political commentators: that a cohesive ruling group persists in the

United States despite the country's size and the diversity of interests within it.

The material for this book was gathered from club members, present and former employees of the clubs, historical archives, and newspapers. Almost all the information presented can be found in scattered public sources, but interviews were essential in making sense out of it. Repeated discussions with two interviewees also enriched the account with colorful details and with a feel for the ethos of the encampments and rides. I am deeply indebted to these people for their help.

The biographical information, which is the systematic core of the book, comes primarily from the years 1965 to 1970. Although post-1970 occupations and appointments are noted for some of the people discussed, I have not tried to take account of deaths, retirements, and changes in occupational status after 1970. For this reason, the account is already history in some sense of the word. However, this presents no problem from my perspective, for the people mentioned are merely exemplars of an ongoing social process. I hope readers will keep this caution in mind when they come across the name of a deceased or retired person who is spoken of as if he were still alive or active in his business or profession.

My primary research assistants for this project were Joel Schaffer, Michael Spiro, and Lisa Young, who carried out the studies of the social, economic, and political connections of members and guests. They also combed newspaper and magazine sources for relevant information. Their detailed labors are gratefully acknowledged, and a special thanks is added to Lisa Young for her fine drawings, which enhance this book.

I also want to express my thanks for the helpful hints of

writer John Van der Zee, whose research efforts on the first retreat I discuss—the Bohemian Grove—came to my attention as I was finishing my research and beginning to write. Although we have not compared notes, he was helpful to me in several ways, as I hope I was to him in certain small details. His book on the Bohemian Grove is entitled *Power at Ease: Inside the Greatest Men's Party on Earth* (Harcourt Brace Jovanovich, 1974).

My research on the second retreat discussed, the Rancheros Visitadores, was aided in its initial stages by the work of Michael Williams, "Los Rancheros Visitadores," a paper for my graduate sociology seminar on the American upper class at the University of California, Santa Barbara, in the fall of 1970. After the chapter was written, I learned further useful details from the undergraduate research work conducted by Peggy Rodgers and Donna Beck of the University of California, Santa Barbara, and I am grateful to them for sharing their findings with me.

As in the past, friends and colleagues have saved me from a multitude of sins, both substantive and stylistic. In this instance, my most helpful reader was my major informant, who unfortunately must remain nameless. Other readers with helpful suggestions were Richie Zweigenhaft, a social psychologist at the University of California, Santa Cruz, and Cynthia Merman, my editor at Harper & Row.

My thanks, finally, to the Torchbook Department of Harper & Row, and to the Research Committee of the Academic Senate, University of California, Santa Cruz, for the financial support that made this project possible, and to Mrs. Charlotte Cassidy, Cowell College, University of California, Santa Cruz, for typing the final manuscript with her usual careful correction of grammatical and spelling errors.

G.W.D.

University of California
Santa Cruz, California
June 29, 1973

The Bohemian Grove
and Other Retreats

1

The Bohemian Grove

The Cremation of Care

Picture yourself comfortably seated in a beautiful open-air dining hall in the midst of twenty-seven hundred acres of giant California redwoods. It is early evening and the clear July air is still pleasantly warm. Dusk has descended, you have finished a sumptuous dinner, and you are sitting quietly with your drink and your cigar, listening to nostalgic welcoming speeches and enjoying the gentle light and the eerie shadows that are cast by the two-stemmed gaslights flickering softly at each of the several hundred outdoor banquet tables.

You are part of an assemblage that has been meeting in this redwood grove sixty-five miles north of San Francisco for nearly a hundred years. It is not just any assemblage, for you are a captain of industry, a well-known television star, a banker, a famous artist, or maybe a member of the President's Cabinet. You are one of fifteen hundred men gathered together from all over the country for the annual encampment of the rich and the famous at the Bohemian Grove. And you are about to take part in a strange ceremony that has marked every Bohemian Grove gathering since 1880. You are about to be initiated into the encampment by the Cremation of Care.

Out of the shadows on one of the hillsides near the dining circle there come the low, sad sounds of a funeral dirge. As you turn your head in its direction you faintly see the outlines of men dressed in pointed red hoods and red flowing robes. Some of the men are playing the funereal music; others are carrying long torches whose flames are a spectacular sight against the darkened forest.

As the procession approaches the dining circle, the dim figures become more distinct, and attention fixes on several men not previously noticed who are carrying a large wooden box. Upon closer inspection the box turns out to be an open coffin, and in that coffin is a body, a human body—real enough to be lifelike at a glance, but only an imitation, made of black muslin wrapped around a wooden skeleton. This is the body of Care, symbolizing the concerns and woes that important men supposedly must bear in their daily lives. It is Dull Care that is to be cremated this first Saturday night of the two-week encampment of the Bohemian Grove.

The cortege now trails slowly past the dining area, and the men in the dining circle fall into line behind the hooded priests and pallbearers, following the body of Care toward its ultimate destination. The entire parade (all white, mostly elderly) makes its way along a road leading to a picturesque little lake that is yet another of the sylvan sights the Bohemian Grove has to offer.

It takes the communicants about five minutes to make their march to this new setting. Once at the lake the priests and the body of Care go off to the right, in the direction of a very large altar which faces the lake. The followers, talking quietly and remarking on the once-again-perfect Grove weather, move to the left so they can observe the ceremony from a green meadow

2

on the other side of the lake. They will be about fifty to a hundred yards from the altar, which looms skyward thirty to forty feet and reveals itself to be in the form of a huge Owl, whose cement shell is mottled with primeval green mosses.

While the spectators seat themselves across the lake, the priests and their entourage continue for another two or three hundred yards beyond the altar to a boat landing. There the bier is carefully transferred onto the Ferry of Care, which will carry the body to the altar later in the ceremony. The ferry loaded, the torches are extinguished and the music ends. The attention of the spectators on the other side of the lake slowly drifts back to the Owl shrine; it is illuminated by a gentle flame from the Lamp of Fellowship which sits at its base.

People who have seen the ceremony before nudge you to keep your eye on the large redwood next to the Owl. Moments later an offstage chorus of "woodland voices" begins to sing. Then a spotlight illuminates the tree you've been watching, and there emerges from it a hamadryad, a "tree spirit," whose life, according to Greek mythology, is intimately bound up with the tree in which it lives. The hamadryad begins to sing, telling the supplicants that beauty and strength and peace are theirs as long as the trees of the Grove are there. It sings of the "temple-aisles of the wood" that are made for "your delight," and implores the Bohemians to "burn away the sorrows of yesterday" and to "cast your grief to the fires and be strong with the holy trees and the spirit of the Grove."[1]

With the end of this uplifting song, the hamadryad returns to its tree, the chorus silences, and the light on the tree fades

1. Charles K. Field, *The Cremation of Care* (1946, 1953), for these and following quotes. A copy of this small pamphlet can be found in the Bancroft Library, University of California, Berkeley.

3

out. Only natural illumination from the moon and stars remains, and it is time for the high priest and his many assistants to enter the large area in front of the Owl. "The Owl is in his leafy temple," intones the high priest. "Let all within the Grove be reverent before him." He beseeches the spectators to be inspired and awed by their surroundings, noting that this is Bohemia's shrine. Then he invokes the motto of the club, "Weaving spiders, come not here!"—which is a line from Shakespeare's *A Midsummer Night's Dream.* It is supposed to warn members not to discuss business and worldly concerns, but only the arts, literature, and other pleasures, within the portals of Bohemia.

The priest next walks down three large steps to the edge of the lake. There he makes a flowery speech about the ripple of waters, the song of birds, the forest floor, and evening's cool kiss. Again he calls on the members to forsake their usual concerns: "Shake off your sorrows with the City's dust and scatter to the winds the cares of life." A second and third priest then recall to memory deceased friends who loved the Bohemian Grove, and the high priest makes yet another effusive speech, the gist of it being that "Great Nature" is a "refuge for the weary heart" and a "balm for breasts that have been bruised."

A brief song is sung by the chorus and suddenly the high priest proclaims: "Our funeral pyre awaits the corpse of Care!" A horn is sounded at the boat landing. Anon, the Ferry of Care, with its beautifully ornamented frontispiece, begins its brief passage to the foot of the shrine. Its trip is accompanied by the music of a barcarole—a barcarole being the song of Venetian gondoliers as they pole you through the canals of Venice. As one listens to the barcarole, it becomes even clearer that many little extra touches have been added by the Bohemians who have lovingly developed this ritual over its ninety-four-year history.

The bier arrives at the steps of the altar. The high priest inveighs against Dull Care, the archenemy of Beauty. He shouts, "Bring fire," and the torchbearers (eighteen strong) enter. Then the acolytes quickly seize the coffin, lift it high above their heads, and carry it triumphantly to the pyre in front of the mighty Owl. It seems that Care is about to be consumed by flames.

But not yet. Suddenly there is a great clap of thunder and a rush of wind. Peals of loud, ugly laughter come ringing down from a hill above the lake. A dead tree is illuminated in the middle of the hillside, and Care himself bellows forth with a thundering blast:

"Fools! Fools! Fools! When will ye learn that me ye cannot slay? Year after year ye burn me in this Grove, lifting your puny shouts of triumph to the stars. But when again ye turn your feet toward the marketplace, am I not waiting for you, as of old? Fools! Fools! To dream ye conquer Care!"

The high priest is taken aback by this impressive outburst, but not completely humbled. He replies that it is not all a dream, that he and his friends know they will have to face Care when their holiday is over. They are happy that the good fellowship created by the Bohemian Grove is able to banish Care even for a short time. So the high priest tells Care, "We shall burn thee once again this night and in the flames that eat thine effigy we'll read the sign: Midsummer sets us free."

Dull Care, however, is having none of this. He tells the high priest in no uncertain terms that priestly fires are not going to do him in. "I spit upon your fire," he roars, and with that there is a great explosion and all the torches are immediately extinguished. The only light remaining comes from the small flame in the Lamp of Fellowship.

Things are clearly at an impasse. Care may win out after all. There is only one thing to do: turn to the great Owl, the totem animal of Bohemia, chosen as the group's symbol primarily for its mortal wisdom—and only secondarily for its discreet silence and its nightly prowling. The high priest falls to his knees and lifts his arms toward the shrine. "O thou, great symbol of all mortal wisdom," he cries. "Owl of Bohemia, we do beseech thee, grant us thy counsel!"

The inspirational music of the "Fire Finale" now begins, and an aura of light glows about the Owl's head. The Owl is going to rise to the occasion! After a pause, the sagacious bird finally speaks. No fire, he tells the assembled faithful, can drive out Care if that fire comes from the mundane world, where it is fed by the hates of men. There is only one fire that can overcome the great enemy Care, and that, of course, is the flame which burns in the Lamp of Fellowship on the Altar of Bohemia. "Hail, Fellowship," he concludes, "and thou, Dull Care, begone!"

With that, Care is on his way out. The light dies from the dead tree. The high priest leaps to his feet and bounds up the steps, snatches a burned-out torch from one of the bearers, and relights it from the flame of the Lamp of Fellowship. Just as quickly he ignites the funeral pyre and triumphantly hurls the torch into the blaze.

The orchestral music in the background intensifies as the flames leap higher and higher. The chorus sings loudly about Dull Care, archenemy of Beauty, calling on the winds to make merry with his dust. "Hail, Fellowship," they sing, echoing the Owl. "Begone, Dull Care! Midsummer sets us free!" The wailing voice of Care gives its last gasps, the music gets even louder, and fireworks light the sky and fill the Grove with the reverberations of great explosions. The band, appropriately enough, strikes up "There'll Be a Hot Time in the Old Town Tonight." Care has been banished, but only with a cast of 250 elders, priests, torchbearers, shore patrols, fire tenders, production managers, and woodland voices.

As this climax approaches, some fifty minutes after the march began, the quiet onlookers on the other side of the lake begin to come alive. After all, it is a night for rejoicing. The men begin to shout, to sing, to hug each other, and dance around. They have been freed by their priests and their Owl for some good old-fashioned hell raising. They couldn't be happier if they were back in college and their fraternity had won an intramural football championship.

Now the ceremony is over. The revelers, initiated into the carefree attitude of the Bohemian Grove, break up into small groups as they return to the camps that crowd next to each other in the central area of the Grove. It will be a night of storytelling and drinking for the men of Bohemia as they sit about their campfires or wander from camp to camp, renewing old friendships and making new ones. They will be far away from their responsibilities as the decision makers and opinion molders of corporate America.

Jinks High and Jinks Low

The Cremation of Care is the most spectacular event of the midsummer retreat that members and guests of San Francisco's Bohemian Club have taken every year since 1878. However, there are several other entertainments in store. Before the

Bohemians return to the everyday world, they will be treated to plays, variety shows, song fests, shooting contests, art exhibits, swimming, boating, and nature rides. Of all these delights, the most elaborate are the two Jinks: High Jinks and Low Jinks.

Among Bohemians, planned entertainment of any real magnitude is called a Jinks. This nomenclature extends from the earliest days of the club, when its members were searching for precedents and traditions to adopt from the literature and entertainment of other times and other places. In the case of Jinks, they had found a Scottish word which denotes, generally speaking, a frolic, although it also was used in the past to refer to a drinking bout which involved a matching of wits to see who paid for the drinks. Bohemian Club historiographers, however, claim the word was gleaned from a more respectable source, *Guy Mannering*, a novel by Sir Walter Scott; there the High Jinks are a more elevated occasion, with drinking only a subsidiary indulgence.[2]

In any event, the early Jinks at the Grove slowly developed into more and more elaborate entertainments. By 1902 the High Jinks had become what it is today, a grandiose, operetta-like extravaganza that is written and produced by club members for its one-time-only presentation in the Grove. The High Jinks, presented on the Friday night of the last weekend, is considered the most important formal event of the encampment.

Most of the plays written for the High Jinks have a mythical or fantasy theme, although a significant minority have a historical setting. Any moral messages center on inevitable human frailty, not social injustice. There is no spoofing of the powers-that-be at a High Jinks; it is strictly a highbrow occasion. A

2. Robert H. Fletcher, *The Annals of the Bohemian Club* (San Francisco: Hicks-Judd Company, 1900), Vol. I, 1872–80, p. 34.

few titles give the flavor: *The Man in the Forest* (1902), *The Cave Man* (1910), *The Fall of Ug* (1913), *The Rout of the Philistines* (1922), *The Golden Feather* (1939), *Johnny Apple-seed* (1946), *A Gest of Robin Hood* (1954), *Rip Van Winkle* (1960), and *The Bonnie Cravat* (1970).

A priest, of all unlikely people, holds the honor of being the only person to be the subject of two Grove plays. He is the Patron Saint of Bohemia, Saint John of Nepomuck (pronounced NAY-po-muk), a man who lived in the thirteenth century in the real Bohemia that is now part of Czechoslovakia. Saint John received his unique distinction among latter-day Bohe-mians in 1882, when his sad but courageous story was told in a jinks "sired" (the club argot for master of ceremonies) by the poet Charles Warren Stoddard.

Saint John was a cutup in his youth, but had forsaken ephemeral pleasures—or at least most of them—for the priest-hood. One of his first assignments was as a tutor to the heir apparent to the kingship of Bohemia. John soon became fast friends with the fun-loving prince, often joining him in his spirited and amorous adventures. When the prince became king, he made Saint John the court confessor.

All went well for Saint John until the king began to suspect that his beautiful queen was having a love affair with the Margrave of Moravia. To allay his suspicions, the king naturally turned to his loyal friend and teacher, Saint John of Nepomuck, demanding that this former companion in many revelries reveal to him the most intimate confessions of the queen. Saint John refused. The king pleaded, but to no avail. Then the king threatened; this had no effect either. Finally, in a fit of rage, he ordered Saint John hurled into the river to drown. John chose to die rather than reveal a woman's secrets. Here, truly, was a remarkable fellow, and his story appealed mightily to the San Francisco Bohemians of the nineteenth century.

Several months after the poet Stoddard introduced Saint John to his fellow Bohemians there arrived at the clubhouse in San Francisco a small statue of Saint John from faraway Czechoslovakia. It seems one of the people present for Stoddard's talk had been Count Joseph Oswald Von Thun of Czechoslovakia, who had been much taken by the club and its appreciation of his fellow countryman. Upon his return to Czechoslovakia he had commissioned a woodcarver to make a replica of the statue of Saint John which adorns the bridge in Prague near the place of his drowning.

This unexpected gift still guards the library room in the Bohemians' large club building in San Francisco—except during the encampment at the Grove, that is. For that event the statue is carefully transported to a hallowed tree near the center of the Grove, where Saint John, with his forefinger carefully sealing his lips, can be a saintly reminder of the need for discretion.

The legend surrounding Saint John of Nepomuck became part of the oral tradition of the Bohemian Club. New members inevitably hear the story when they happen upon the statue while being shown around the city clubhouse or the Grove. But oral tradition is not enough for a patron saint, and the good man's legend was therefore enacted in a Grove play in 1921 under the title *St. John of Nepomuck*. It was retold in 1969 by a different author under the title *St. John of Bohemia*.

How good are the Grove plays? "Pretty darn good," says one member who knows theater. He thinks maybe one in ten High Jinks would be a commercial success if produced for outside audiences. Another member is not so sure about their general appeal. "They're damned fine productions," he claims, "but they are so geared to the special features of a Grove encampment, and so full of schmaltz and nostalgia, that it's hard to say how well they'd go over with ordinary audiences."

Whatever the quality, the plays are enormously elaborate productions, with huge casts, large stage sets, much singing, and dazzling lighting effects. "Hell, most stages wouldn't hold a Grove production," said our second informant. "That Grove stage is about ten thousand square feet, and there are all sorts of pathways leading into it from the hillside behind it. Not to mention the little clearings on the hillside which are used to great effect in some plays."

A cast for a typical Grove play easily runs to seventy-five or one hundred people. Add in the orchestra, the stagehands, the carpenters who make the sets, and other supporting personnel, and over three hundred people are involved in creating the High Jinks each year. Preparations begin a year in advance, with rehearsals occurring two or three times a week in the month before the encampment, and nightly in the week before the play.

Costs are on the order of $20,000 to $30,000 per High Jinks, a large amount of money for a one-night production which does not have to pay a penny for salaries (the highest cost in any commercial production). "And the costs are talked about, too," reports my second informant. " 'Hey, did you hear the High Jinks will cost $25,000 this year?' one of them will say to another. The expense of the play is one way they can relate to its worth."

One person clearly impressed by a Grove play and its costs was Harold L. Ickes, the outspoken Secretary of the Interior during the New Deal era. Unbeknown to most people at the time, Ickes was keeping a detailed diary of his experiences. *The Secret Diary of Harold L. Ickes* appeared in 1953, and it contained, among other interesting observations about the Bohemian Grove, the following account of the play for 1934:

> But the thing that made the greatest impression on me was the play that night. The theater is an open-air one in a natural opening, surrounded by towering sequoias. The stage is at the foot of a sharp hill. The hill is covered with trees and undergrowth and the proscenium arch of the stage consists of two giant sequoias with intermingled tops. It was one of the most impressive and magnificent settings I have ever seen. The play that night was a serious one, the theme being the conversion of the old Irish Druids by St. Patrick. It had been written by the late Professor James Stephens, an Englishman, who had been a member of the English faculty at the University of California. All the parts were taken by the members of the Bohemian Club and the acting could not have been better if it had been done by professionals; in fact, I doubt whether it would have been so well done. It was very impressive to see the actors carrying torches and following the trails down the hillside. The costuming and the lighting were very well done. I was told that the lighting for that one play cost $25,000, and certainly it would have been difficult to improve upon it.[3]

The High Jinks is the pride of the Grove, but a little highbrow stuff goes a long way among clubmen, even clubmen who like to think of themselves as cultured. From the early beginnings of the club, the High Jinks has been counterbal-

3. Harold L. Ickes, *The Secret Diary of Harold L. Ickes, Vol. 1. The First Thousand Days, 1933–36.* (New York: Simon and Schuster, 1953), pp. 178–79. I am grateful to my friend and colleague, historian George W. Baer, for calling this passage to my attention.

anced by the more slapstick and ribald fun of Low Jinks. For many years the Low Jinks were basically haphazard and extemporaneous, but slowly they too became more elaborate and professional as the Grove grew from a few campers on a weekend holiday to a full-blown two-week encampment which requires year-round planning and maintenance. Now the Low Jinks is a specially-written musical comedy requiring almost as much attention and concern as the High Jinks. Personnel requirements are slightly less—perhaps 200–250 people to the 300–350 needed for High Jinks. Costs also are slightly lower— $5,000 to $10,000 per year versus $20,000 or more for a High Jinks.

The subject matter of the Low Jinks is very different from that of the High Jinks. The title of the first formal Low Jinks in 1924 was *The Lady of Monte Rio,* which every good Bohemian would immediately recognize as an allusion to the ladies of the evening who are available in certain inns and motels near the Grove. The 1968 Low Jinks concerned *The Sin of Ophelia Grabb,* who lived with Letchwell Lear in unwedded bliss even though she was the daughter of the mayor of Shady Corners. *Thrice Knightly,* another recent Low Jinks, also needs no explanation, especially to old fraternity boys who know that "once a king always a king, but once a knight is enough." And *Socially Prominent,* the 1971 Low Jinks, was unsparingly funny about the High Society whence many members originate.

Little Friday Night, Big Saturday Night

The Cremation of Care, the High Jinks, and the Low Jinks are productions involving hundreds of ordinary Bohemian Club members. They require planning, coordination, and money,

13

and Bohemians are proud of the fact that they are part of a club which creates its own theatrical enjoyments. However, the Bohemians are not averse to enjoying professional entertainment by stars of stage, screen, and television. For this, there are the Little Friday Night and the Big Saturday Night.

The Little Friday Night is held on the second weekend of the encampment. The Big Saturday Night is on the third weekend—it closes the encampment. Both are shows made up of acts put on by famous stars. It is here that members may hear jokes that fellow Bohemians Art Linkletter, Edgar Bergen, and Dan Rowan never tell on television, or enjoy songs that Phil Harris doesn't do in the nightclubs of Lake Tahoe and Reno. The host for the evening may be Ray Bolger, one of the most active entertainers in Bohemia, or Andy Devine, Ralph Edwards, or Lowell Thomas. One of the vocalists might be Bing Crosby, another, Dennis Day. For musical numbers there is Les Brown —or perhaps Raymond Hackett or George Shearing. Celebrity members are supplemented by celebrity guests. Milton Berle entertained one year. Jerry Van Dyke was part of the Big Saturday Night in 1970. Victor Borge was a recent guest. So were trumpeters Al Hirt and Harry James.

All of this talent is free, of course. No one would think of asking for money to perform for such a select audience, and if anyone should think to ask, he immediately would be disinvited. People are supposed to understand it is an honor to entertain those in attendance at the Bohemian Grove.

Lakeside Talks

Entertainment is not the only activity at the Bohemian Grove. For a little change of pace, there is intellectual stimulation and political enlightenment every day at 12:30 P.M. Since 1932 the meadow from which people view the Cremation of Care also has been the setting for informal talks and briefings by people as varied as Dwight David Eisenhower (before he was President), Herman Wouk (author of *The Caine Mutiny*), Bobby Kennedy (while he was Attorney General), and Neil Armstrong (after he returned from the moon).

Cabinet officers, politicians, generals, and governmental advisers are the rule rather than the exception for Lakeside Talks, especially on weekends. Equally prominent figures from the worlds of art, literature, and science are more likely to make their appearance during the weekdays of the encampment, when Grove attendance may drop to four or five hundred (many of the members only come up for one week or for the weekends because they cannot stay away from their corporations and law firms for the full two weeks).

Members vary as to how interesting and informative they find the Lakeside Talks. Some find them useful, others do not, probably depending on their degree of familiarity with the topic being discussed. It is fairly certain that no inside or secret information is divulged, but a good feel for how a particular problem will be handled is likely to be communicated. Whatever the value of the talks, most members think there is something very nice about hearing official government policy, orthodox big-business ideology, and new scientific information from a fellow Bohemian or one of his guests in an informal atmosphere where no reporters are allowed to be present.

One person who seems to find Lakeside Talks a useful forum is President Richard M. Nixon, a Bohemian Club member since 1953. A speech he gave at the Grove in 1967 was the basis for a public speech he gave a few months later. Richard J. Whalen, one of Nixon's speech writers in the late sixties, tells the story as follows:

> He would speak at the Hoover Institution, before a conference on the fiftieth anniversary of the Bolshevik revolution. "I don't want it to be the typical anti-Communist harangue—you know, there's Nixon again. Try to *lift* it. I want to take a *sophisticated* hard line. I'd like to be very fair and objective about their achievements—in fifty years they've come from a cellar conspiracy to control of half the world. But I also want to underline the horrible costs of their methods and system." He handed me a copy of his speech the previous summer at Bohemian Grove, telling me to take it as a model for outlining the changes in the Communist world and the changing U.S. Policy toward the Soviet Union.[4]

The ease with which the Bohemian Grove is able to attract famous speakers for no remuneration other than the amenities of the encampment attests to the high esteem in which the club is held in the higher circles. Down through the years the Lakeside podium has hosted such luminaries as Lee DuBridge (science), David Sarnoff (business), Wernher von Braun (space technology), Senator Robert Taft, Lucius Clay (military and business), Earl Warren (Supreme Court), former California Republican Governor Goodwin J. Knight, and former California Democratic Governor Pat Brown. For many years former

4. Richard J. Whalen, *Catch the Falling Flag: A Republican's Challenge to His Party* (Boston: Houghton Mifflin, 1972), p. 25. Earlier in this book, on page 4, Whalen reports that his own speech in 1969 at the Bohemian Grove, which concerned the U.S.-Soviet nuclear balance, was distributed by President Nixon to cabinet members and other administration officials with a presidential memorandum commending it as an "excellent analysis." I am grateful to sociologist Richard Hamilton of McGill University for bringing this material to my attention.

16

President Herbert C. Hoover, who joined the club in 1913, was a regular feature of the Lakeside Talks, with the final Saturday afternoon being reserved for his anachronistic counsel.

Politicians apparently find the Lakeside Talks especially attractive. "Giving a Lakeside" provides them with a means for personal exposure without officially violating the injunction "Weaving spiders, come not here." After all, Bohemians rationalize, a Lakeside Talk is merely an informal chat by a friend of the family.

Some members, at least, know better. They realize that the Grove is an ideal off-the-record atmosphere for sizing up politicians. "Well, of course when a politician comes here, we all get to see him, and his stock in trade is his personality and his ideas," a prominent Bohemian told a *New York Times* reporter who was trying to cover Nelson Rockefeller's 1963 visit to the Grove for a Lakeside Talk. The journalist went on to note that the midsummer encampments "have long been a major showcase where leaders of business, industry, education, the arts, and politics can come to examine each other."[5]

Speakers for the 1970 encampment were an exceptionally impressive group. Indeed, the program was so heavily laced with governmental appointees that protests were voiced by some members. Following is the main portion of it for that year in the order it appears in the club's yearly *Report of the President and the Treasurer.*

5. Wallace Turner, "Rockefeller Faces Scrutiny of Top Californians: Governor to Spend Weekend at Bohemian Grove among State's Establishment" (*New York Times,* July 26, 1963), p. 30. In 1964 Senator Barry Goldwater appeared at the Grove as a guest of retired General Albert C. Wedemeyer and Herbert Hoover, Jr. For that story see Wallace Turner, "Goldwater Spending Weekend in Camp at Bohemian Grove" (*New York Times,* July 31, 1964), p. 10.

Hardin B. Jones
   Professor of Medical Physics and Physiology, University of California, Berkeley
Rudolph A. Peterson
   President of the Bank of America
Norman H. Strouse
   Renowned book collector, retired President of J. Walter Thompson Advertising Agency
Robley C. Williams
   Professor of Biophysics, University of California, Berkeley
Frank Shakespeare
   Director, United States Information Agency
Ernest L. Wilkinson
   President, Brigham Young University
Henry Kissinger
   President Nixon's foreign policy adviser
Melvin Laird
   Secretary of Defense
Edward Cole
   President of General Motors
Earl C. Bolton
   Vice President, University of California, Berkeley
Gunnar Johansen
   Professor of Music, University of Wisconsin
Russell E. Train
   Chairman, Council on Environment Quality
Emil Mosbacher
   Chief of Protocol, State Department
William P. Rogers
   Secretary of State
Neil Armstrong
   Astronaut

For 1971, President Nixon was to be the featured Lakeside speaker. However, when newspaper reporters learned that the President planned to disappear into a redwood grove for an off-the-record speech to some of the most powerful men in America, they objected loudly and vowed to make every effort to cover the event. The flap caused the club considerable embarrassment, and after much hemming and hawing back and forth, the club leaders asked the President to cancel his scheduled appearance. A White House press secretary then announced that the President had decided not to appear at the Grove rather than risk the tradition that speeches there are strictly off the public record.[6]

However, the President was not left without a final word to his fellow Bohemians. In a telegram to the president of the club, which now hangs at the entrance to the reading room in the San Francisco clubhouse, he expressed his regrets at not being able to attend. He asked the club president to continue to lead people into the woods, adding that he in turn would redouble his efforts to lead people out of the woods. He also noted that, while anyone could aspire to be President of the United States, only a few could aspire to be president of the Bohemian Club.

Cliff Dwellers, Moonshiners, and Silverado Squatters

Not all the entertainment at the Bohemian Grove takes place under the auspices of the committee in charge of special events. The Bohemians and their guests are divided into camps which

6. James M. Naughton, "Nixon Drops Plan for Coast Speech" (*New York Times,* July 31, 1971), p. 11.

evolved slowly over the years as the number of people on the retreat grew into the hundreds and then the thousands. These camps have become a significant center of enjoyment during the encampment.

At first the camps were merely a place in the woods where a half-dozen to a dozen friends would pitch their tents. Soon they added little amenities like their own special stove or a small permanent structure. Then there developed little camp "traditions" and endearing camp names like Cliff Dwellers, Moonshiners, Silverado Squatters, Woof, Zaca, Toyland, Sun-dodgers, and Land of Happiness. The next steps were special emblems, a handsome little lodge or specially constructed tepees, a permanent bar, and maybe a grand piano.[7] Today there are 129 camps of varying sizes, structures, and statuses. Most have between 10 and 30 members, but there are one or two with about 125 members and several with less than 10. A majority of the camps are strewn along what is called the River Road, but some are huddled in other areas within five or ten minutes of the center of the Grove.

The entertainment at the camps is mostly informal and impromptu. Someone will decide to bring together all the jazz musicians in the Grove for a special session. Or maybe all the artists or writers will be invited to a luncheon or a dinner at a camp. Many camps have their own amateur piano players and informal musical and singing groups which perform for the rest of the members.

But the joys of the camps are not primarily in watching or

7. There is a special moisture-proof building at the Grove to hold the dozens of expensive Steinway pianos belonging to the club and various camps.

listening to performances. Other pleasures are created within them. Some camps become known for their gastronomical specialties, such as a particular drink or a particular meal. The Jungle Camp features mint juleps, Halcyon has a three-foot-high martini maker constructed out of chemical glassware. At the Owl's Nest it's the gin-fizz breakfast—about a hundred people are invited over one morning during the encampment for eggs Benedict, gin fizzes, and all the trimmings.

Poison Oak is famous for its Bulls' Balls Lunch. Each year a cattle baron from central California brings a large supply of testicles from his newly castrated herds for the delectation of Poison Oakers and their guests. No one goes away hungry. Bulls' balls are said to be quite a treat. Meanwhile, one small camp has a somewhat different specialty, which is not necessarily known to members of every camp. It houses a passé pornographic collection which is more amusing than erotic. Connoisseurs do not consider it a great show, but it is an easy way to kill a lazy afternoon.

Almost all camps stress that people from other camps are free to walk in at any time of the day or night. Hospitality and a free drink are the proper form of behavior, and everyone talks about this easy congeniality. Some camps go out of their way to advertise their friendliness. In the little Grove museum featuring birds and mammals from the area, the Rattler's Camp put the following sign above the rattlesnake exhibit: "Anyone looking at this rattlesnake is hereby entitled to a free drink at Rattler's Camp."

A brief history of all the camps is included in the large scrapbooks in the Bohemian Club library room. Most of these histories describe how the camp acquired its name, tell an anecdote or two about the camp or its founders, and then list some of the famous Americans who have been guests there over the generations.

A few camps go so far as to print for the members a history of the camp. The Lost Angels, a camp with a strong Los Angeles contingent, permitted themselves this little indulgence on their fiftieth anniversary in 1958. The history, complete with pictures and membership lists, tells how the founders of the camp broke away from another camp because they felt "lost," only to find themselves half-seriously hassled by the Grove authorities for a campfire that was smoking out fellow Bohemians. The Lost Angels retaliated for this harassment by moving to a somewhat removed hillside, where the next year they built an utterly lavish (by Grove standards) lodge complete with elegant mahogany furniture and special appointments like virgin lambs' wool blankets from the Isle of Wight and lace tablecloths from Ireland. It was a $12,000 joke even in 1908—which is about $50,000 by 1958 standards.

The outlandish Lost Angels camp was a huge success in outraging members of other camps. It caused consternation everywhere, inspiring numerous jokes and jingles which are faithfully preserved in Lost Angels lore. However, the final laugh was on the Lost Angels. When they weren't looking, members of other camps stole everything of value. Lost Angels was happy to return to the plainer and simpler atmosphere that the Grove tries to maintain, but it is still regarded as one of the nicest camps in the Grove.

The camps, then, add another dimension to the activities at the Bohemian Grove. They provide a basis for smaller and less-organized entertainments in an even more intimate atmosphere. They provide an excuse for half-serious rivalries, for practical jokes, for within-group differentiation. "The camps," one former employee told me, "make the Bohemian Grove seem like a college fraternity system transplanted from the campus to the redwoods." "Like an overgrown boy-scout camp," explained another employee, who drives one of the little ʋam buses that travel quietly throughout the Grove for the convenience of those who don't wish to walk.

Other Delights

Formal Grove shows and informal camp shenanigans do not exhaust the possibilities of the Bohemian Grove. Members can find a number of other ways to amuse themselves.

Some wander about quietly, drink in hand, enjoying the redwood trails. Others walk down the River Road to look at the meandering water of the Russian River 150 feet below; often they take the winding path down to the river and its beach, where they sit on the large beach deck, wade in the shallow water along the banks, swim in the specially developed swimming hole, or even paddle out in one of the Grove canoes.

Others can be found taking part in the skeet shooting and trap shooting that are provided. Some take regularly scheduled "rim rides" on Grove buses, journeying to the more distant parts of the Grove's several thousand acres while a tour guide recounts the natural history of the area. Many plan their late-morning visit to the Civic Center (a group of small buildings which serve as message center, barber shop, and drug store) so they can make it to the noon organ concert which is held each day by the lake. (The Bohemian band and the Bohemian orchestra also perform one afternoon concert each during the encampment.)

A pleasant afternoon can be spent at the Ice House, the beautiful redwood building that houses an annual art exhibit made up of paintings, photographs, and sculpture created by Bohemian Club members. Over three hundred original works of art are usually available for viewing.[8] For evenings without large productions, there are less formal Campfire Circle entertainments featuring the band, the orchestra, the chorus, or individual storytellers and entertainers.

Skeet shooting, swimming, art exhibitions—there is plenty to see and do in the Bohemian Grove even when a big production is not being staged. It is truly a place of many delights. But, despite all these attractions, it remains most of all a place to rest and relax in the company of friends.

Jumping the River

Alert readers may have noticed that one pleasure is missing for these hundreds of men in search of a good time. That pleasure is female companionship. For a certain minority of Bohemians—reliable estimates put the figure well below 10 percent—such companionship is a necessity of life they cannot be without. Since women are strictly forbidden to enter the Grove, there is only one thing to do—jump the river.

Now, eager Bohemians do not literally jump or swim across the river. That is only an expression which some Bohemians use for going to one of two nearby towns to find an attractive prostitute at a bar which caters to the Bohemian Grove trade.

There are two little towns near the Grove. One, Monte Rio, is about a mile from the Grove entrance, and has a population of 997. The other, Guerneville, a metropolis of 1,005, is a mile or two from Monte Rio; it has seven or eight bars. In the not

8. And for sale. Painters in particular earn a considerable amount of money through the Bohemian Club. But that is getting ahead of the story.

too distant past there were several bars in both towns which were frequented by Bohemians who had jumped the river. Two or three even had private rooms where people could have their own special parties. But bars come and go, and the scene of the action changes from time to time. In recent years much of the extracurricular activity centered around the Gas House Tavern in Guerneville, where the owner was partial to the Grove to the point of putting Grove scenes on his walls and trying to accumulate Bohemian mementos.

Jumping the river suddenly became a risky sport in 1971. A new sheriff, making good on a clean-government campaign promise, began to crack down on prostitutes. He even hired an undercover agent to help him gain information. The sheriff and his investigators claim to have observed about twenty women turning, on the average, three tricks a night. Contacts, they said, were made in the Gas House Tavern, and the arrangement was consummated in one of the nearby motels or cottages. Some prominent business people, but no politicians, are mentioned in their reports.

The result of these snoopings was the indictment of the Gas House owner for allowing females to solicit acts of prostitution in his place of business. Also indicted were a married couple from San Francisco, who were charged with supplying the prostitutes at a reported fee of $100 to $150 per person. It looked like the county had a very good case, but it went out the window on the first day of the trial when the defense lawyers revealed that the prosecution's star witness, the undercover agent, was herself a former prostitute with an arrest record.

The angry judge immediately declared a mistrial. "I feel that frankly it is incredible that four investigative agencies, the

Sheriff's Office, the District Attorney's investigators, the Attorney General's investigators for the state, and the FBI were unable to locate [a record of] a felony conviction of one of their witnesses," he scolded.[9] The thirty-nine-year-old former prostitute had been suggested to Sonoma County authorities for the undercover role by an FBI agent. When called to the stand, the Sonoma County criminal investigator who hired her said that the FBI man warned him she had been a registered prostitute in Nevada in 1954, but not that she had been convicted of pimping and pandering in California in 1961. Asked why he didn't check further, he replied that he didn't feel the need because prostitution is not illegal in Nevada. A blunder thus spared the Bohemian Grove from having further details of Guerneville prostitution entered into the court records and the newspapers.

River jumping decreased considerably during the 1972 encampment, if we can trust San Francisco *Chronicle* columnist Herb Caen, a man who seems to have excellent sources about the goings-on of San Franciscans. "Fewer prostitutes around the Bohemian Grove than last year," he reported. "The redlighters no longer have the green light after that recent well-publicized trial."[10] Others suspect that the prostitutes keep closer to their motels, with addresses being supplied by knowledgeable bartenders.

Decrease or not, the amount of prostitution around the encampment was always greatly overplayed. As so often in groups of men, with their proclivities toward bragging and

9. Paul Avery, "Mistrial Ordered in Russian River Case" (San Francisco *Chronicle*, March 15, 1972), p. 3.

10. Herb Caen, "The Morning Line" (San Francisco *Chronicle*, July 25, 1972), p. 17.

storytelling, there is more talk than action. Indeed, many people who know only a little about the Grove seem to think it is one big orgy. Members of the Bohemian Club are extremely shy of publicity, and they are especially sensitive on the subject of prostitution around the Grove. They do not like to have the subject raised at all, and when it is discussed, they have every reason to underestimate greatly its prevalence. Nevertheless, their estimates are not much lower than those of more reliable sources—a friend who worked in the Grove parking lot one summer on the midnight to 8 A.M. shift; a former employee inside the camp; and a member who spent many a late night around the Grove entrance.

However, it is not merely outsiders and journalists who talk about prostitution around the Bohemian Grove. The subject also commands bemused attention within the encampment itself. The relatively few incidents are the subject of exaggeration, myth making, and a lot of kidding. The topic is outranked as a subject for light conversation only by remarks about drinking enormous quantities of alcohol and urinating on redwoods. Even a sedate member far removed from high living could recall a story about a foursome chipping in to hire a prostitute for one of their friends on his seventieth birthday. Such a tale may or may not be true, but it is typical of the kind of story that goes around in an idyllic Grove which only lacks for members of the opposite sex.

The Sociology of Bohemia

Beyond noting that Bohemians and their guests are likely to be rich, famous, or politically prominent, the account thus far has provided little systematic indication of their socioeconomic

27

characteristics. It is therefore time to go into more detail about the social, economic, and political connections of the men who come to the Bohemian Grove for a little rest and recreation. A careful study of the 1968 membership list and the 1970 guest list—the only recent lists available to me—reveals the following information.

Geographic Distribution

Men come to the Bohemian Grove from every part of the United States. Forty states and the District of Columbia contributed members and guests. California, as might be expected, supplies a big majority of the campers. New York is second with 133 representatives, followed by Washington (42), Illinois (38), Ohio (28), District of Columbia (27), Hawaii (24), and Texas (20). The areas least represented are the Deep South (South Carolina, Georgia, Alabama, Louisiana, Mississippi, and Arkansas) with 5, and the thinly populated states of the Far West (Montana, Utah, Wyoming, and Idaho) with 7.

Social Standing

There are relatively reliable ways of determining whether or not a person is a member of the social upper class in America. They include a listing in certain social registers and blue books, attendance at one of a few dozen expensive private schools, and membership in one of several dozen exclusive social clubs. I say these means are "relatively reliable" because no social indicators in any aspect of the social sciences are likely to be perfect.

On the one hand, there are going to be mistakes where people identified as members of the upper class by one or another indicator are not in fact members. Such mistakes ("false positives") can occur for a number of reasons. Perhaps the person was among the few who went to a private school on a scholarship. Then too, upper-middle-class sons and daughters of professionals and academics often attend such schools. In the case of the clubs, there is reason to believe they sometimes include people of middle-class backgrounds who have achieved high positions in certain occupations.

Conversely, there will be mistakes where members of the upper class are overlooked ("false negatives")—because there is no social register or blue book for their city, because not all members of the upper class bother to list themselves in available blue books, because they do not admit to their private-school background in biographical sources, or because they do not find pleasure in belonging to clubs. The "false positives" and the "false negatives," then, are likely to cancel each other out.

Perhaps the biggest problem in determining upper-class standing is that the necessary kinds of information are not publicly available on many people. Since prep-school alumni lists and social-club membership lists are hard to obtain, there is no easy way of finding out about the social backgrounds of the many people who are not outstanding enough in their occupations to be listed in one of several *Who's Who* volumes. Thus, social indicators give us only an idea of the degree to which members of the upper class are overrepresented in various social groups, corporations, and governmental agencies.[11]

11. For further discussion of these problems, and a list of social indicators, see G. William Domhoff, *Who Rules America?* (Englewood Cliffs, N.J.: Prentice-Hall, 1967), Chapter 1, and G. William Domhoff, *The Higher Circles* (New York: Random House, 1970), Chapter 1.

As for the Bohemian Club, it has a very large number of members who are designated by two social indicators as members of the uppermost social class. Among the 928 resident members for 1968 (a category which includes all those who live within one hundred air miles of San Francisco and pay full dues and initiation fees), 27 percent are listed in the San Francisco *Social Register*. Considering that only 0.5 percent of the people in San Francisco are listed in the *Social Register*, and that some resident members do not live in San Francisco or its closest suburbs, this is an impressive figure. It is 54 times the number we would expect to find if the club had no particular social class bias.

Resident members were checked against one other social indicator, the Pacific Union Club, the most exclusive gentlemen's club in San Francisco. This comparison revealed that 22 percent of resident Bohemian members are also members of this more exclusive club. Combining the results from these two indicators alone, the *Social Register* and the Pacific Union Club, we can say that 38 percent of the 928 regular resident members belong to the social upper class.

The Bohemian Club also has 411 nonresident members who are considered "regular" members (as opposed to special members who pay lower dues and will be discussed in a moment). Among this group, 45 percent are listed in one of several social registers and blue books that were cross-tabulated. Seventy were listed in the Los Angeles *Blue Book*, 24 in the New York *Social Register*, 12 in the Chicago *Social Register*, and five in the Houston and Philadelphia *Social Registers*.

It would be possible to make time-consuming investigations into the school backgrounds and club memberships of all regular Bohemian Club members, but it is not really necessary. The basic point has been made: the Bohemian Club has an abundance of members with impeccable social credentials.

Corporate Connections

The men of Bohemia are drawn in large measure from the corporate leadership of the United States. They include in their numbers directors from major corporations in every sector of the American economy. An indication of this fact is that one in every five resident members and one in every three nonresident members is found in Poor's *Register of Corporations, Executives, and Directors,* a huge volume which lists the leadership of tens of thousands of companies from every major business field except investment banking, real estate, and advertising.

Even better evidence for the economic prominence of the men under consideration is that at least one officer or director from 40 of the 50 largest industrial corporations in America was present, as a member or a guest, on the lists at our disposal. Only Ford Motor Company and Western Electric were missing among the top 25! Similarly, we found that officers and directors from 20 of the top 25 commercial banks (including all of the 15 largest) were on our lists. Men from 12 of the first 25 life-insurance companies were in attendance (8 of these 12 were from the top 10). Other business sectors were represented somewhat less: 10 of 25 in transportation, 8 of 25 in utilities, 7 of 25 in conglomerates, and only 5 of 25 in retailing. More generally, of the top-level businesses ranked by *Fortune* for 1969 (the top 500 industrials, the top 50 commercial banks, the top 50 life-insurance companies, the top 50 transportation companies, the top 50 utilities, the top 50 retailers, and the top 47 conglomerates), *29 percent of these 797 corporations were "represented" by at least 1 officer or director.*

Political Contributions

Judging by campaign contributions, Bohemians and their guests, for all their pretensions about being free and imaginative spirits, are overwhelmingly devotees of the unfree and unimaginative Republican party. Two hundred twenty-three Bohemians and their guests are on record as giving $500 or more each to national-level politicians in 1968—200 of them (90 percent) gave to Republicans. (Four others gave to members of both parties.) This Republican fixation is in keeping with our previous findings on the California Club in Los Angeles (154 Republican donors, five Democratic donors), the Pacific Union in San Francisco (84 Republican angels, five Democratic donors), and the Detroit Club in Detroit (105 Republicans, five Democrats).[12] It also is in line with the overwhelming preference for Republican candidates uncovered in studies of campaign contributions by corporate executives.[13]

Associate Members

There are several hundred members of the Bohemian Club who are not socially prominent, not corporation directors, not political fat cats. The largest number of people in this "other" group are the talented Bohemians who are "associate" members

12. G. William Domhoff, *Fat Cats and Democrats* (Englewood Cliffs, N.J.: Prentice-Hall, 1972), pp. 61–62.
13. Herbert E. Alexander, *Money in Politics* (Washington, D.C.: Public Affairs Press, 1972), Chapter 9, for summary and references.

of the club. They are the artists, writers, musicians, actors, and singers who are primarily responsible for the Grove entertainments. It is their presence (at greatly reduced dues) which makes the Bohemian Club unique among high-status clubs in America. The great majority of exclusive social clubs are restricted to rich men and high-level employees in the organizations which rich men control. Only a few, such as the Century in New York and the Tavern in Boston, are like the Bohemian Club in bringing together authors and artists with bankers and businessmen. No other club, however, attempts to put on a program of entertainments and encampments.

Many associate members are not full-time practitioners of their arts. They are instead former professionals, or people good enough to consider becoming professionals, who work at a variety of middle-class occupations. They are insurance salesmen, architects, small businessmen, publishing representatives, advertising directors, and stock brokers, happy to have a social setting within which to exercise their talents on a part-time basis.

Professional Members

The bylaws of the Bohemian Club ensure that at least one hundred of the members of the club shall be professional members. These are people "connected professionally" with literature, art, music, or drama. It is this category which includes Edgar Bergen, Bing Crosby, Tennessee Ernie Ford, George Gobel, Dick Martin, and other "stars." It also includes many people who have graduated from associate membership because they now can afford regular dues or because they wish to take a less-active role in plays and other productions.

Faculty Members

Another special category of Bohemians is that of faculty member. These men are primarily professors and administrators at Stanford University and the various branches of the University of California. However, there is also Lee A. DuBridge, former president of the California Institute of Technology; Grayson Kirk, president of Columbia University; Charles E. Odegaard, president of the University of Washington; Glenn S. Dumke, chancellor of the California State University and College System; Norman Topping, president of the University of Southern California; Glenn T. Seaborg, chairman of the Atomic Energy Commission; and Bayless Manning, former dean of the Stanford Law School, now president of the Council on Foreign Relations in New York.

Many other prominent administrators and professors could be cited, for this group is the most prestigious in the club in terms of honors and positions. Out of ninety-four faculty members, sixty-six are in *Who's Who in America.*

The Camps

Although the official theory about Grove camps stresses their essential equality, there are in fact differences among them. Some, such as Lost Angels and Santa Barbara, have a geographical bias to their membership. Others are characterized by the occupations and professions of their members.

The most specialized camps in terms of membership tend to be made up of the singers, musicians, and other performers who are there to entertain the "regular" members. Aviary, the largest camp, is comprised almost exclusively of associate members who are part of the chorus. Tunerville is the camp for members of the club orchestra. The Band Camp is for members of the band. Monkey Block, named after a famous artists' colony in old San Francisco, has a preponderance of artist members. There are, however, artists in several camps other than Monkey Block, and writers and actors are spread out into many different camps where they share tents or tepees with regular members.

Faculty members are distributed among twenty-eight camps. Most of these camps have only one or two faculty members, but two camps, Sons of Toil and Swagatom, have a majority of university types among their membership. Wayside Lodge, with six faculty members, is known as a hangout for scientists.

The businessmen, bankers, lawyers, and politicians of the club are housed among many camps, sometimes with a few "talented" Bohemians sprinkled among them. However, a handful of camps clearly bring together some of the most influential businessmen and politicians in the country. Far and away the most impressive camp in this category is Mandalay, with its expensive lodgings high up the hillside along the River Road, overlooking the lake. "You don't just walk in there," said one informant. "You are summoned." "A hell of a lot of them bring servants along," noted another. A rundown of Mandalay members as of 1968 can be found in the list below, which reads like an all-star team of the national corporate elite.

MANDALAY CAMP

Francis S. Baer   (*San Francisco*)
   Retired chairman: United California Bank
   Retired director: Union Oil, Jones & Laughlin Steel
Stephen D. Bechtel   (*San Francisco*)
   Chairman: Bechtel Construction
   Director: Morgan Guaranty Trust

37

Atherton Phleger   (*San Francisco*)
   Partner: Brobeck, Phleger, & Harrison (law firm)
   Member: American Bar Association
Herman Phleger   (*San Francisco*)
   Partner: Brobeck, Phleger, & Harrison
   Director: Wells Fargo Bank, Fibreboard Products, Moore Dry Dock Company
   Trustee: Stanford University, Children's Hospital (S.F.)
   Member: American Bar Association
Philip D. Reed   (*New York*)
   Retired chairman: General Electric
   Director: Bankers Trust, American Express, Kraftco, Bigelow-Sanford, Otis Elevator, Metropolitan Life
   Member: Business Council, Committee for Economic Development
Shermer L. Sibley   (*San Francisco*)
   President: Pacific Gas and Electric
   Trustee: Stanford Research Institute, United Bay Area Crusade
Gardiner Symonds   (*Houston*)
   Chairman: Tenneco
   Director: Houston National Bank, Newport News Shipbuilding, Philadelphia Life, Kern County Land Company, Southern Pacific, General Telephone and Electronics
   Trustee: Stanford University, Rice University, Tax Foundation, Stanford Research Institute
   Member: Business Council, Conference Board, Committee for Economic Development
NOTE: Only major directorships, trusteeships, and memberships are listed.

Cave Man is another "heavy" camp. It is most famous among members as the camp of former President Herbert Hoover, but it may be more interesting today as the camp of the present President, Richard M. Nixon. Cave Man seems to be an ideal haven for Nixon. Among its highly conservative members are W. Glenn Campbell, director of the Hoover Institute at Stanford University and a regent of the University of California; Jeremiah Milbank, a major Nixon fund raiser and a director of Commercial Solvents Corporation and Chase Manhattan Bank; Eugene C. Pulliam, a newspaper publisher in Indianapolis and Phoenix; famed aviator Eddie Rickenbacker; and retired General Albert C. Wedemeyer. For balance, there are some less conservative Republicans in the group: Herbert Hoover, Jr., a director of six corporations until his death in 1969; Lowell Thomas, the newscaster; Lowell Thomas, Jr., a director of the Alaska State Bank; and J. E. Wallace Sterling, chancellor of Stanford University.[14]

The Guests

The 1970 Grove guest list is probably the most fascinating document available concerning the sociology of Bohemia. It reveals the guest, his host, and the camp at which he is staying. If such lists were available for a lengthy time span, they would provide the basis for an intimate understanding of the cliques and friendship patterns within the country's ruling circles. As it is, this one list tantalizes us with hypotheses and possibilities.

There were 341 guests at the 1970 encampment. They came from all over the United States (34 states), as well as from Mexico (6), Japan (3), and Spain, the Philippines, England,

14. Sterling has been a very active member. For many years he was in charge of Preachers' Sons' Night, when the sons of ministers are supposed to give speeches and provide entertainment.

40

Switzerland, Austria, Sweden, and Hong Kong (one each). The greatest number were from New York City (79) and Washington, D.C. (25). Some of the pairings are what we might expect. Louis Lundborg, chairman of the Bank of America, had as his guest Gaylord A. Freeman, chairman of the First National Bank of Chicago. David M. Kennedy, former chairman of the Continental Illinois Bank and Trust Company, then serving as Secretary of the Treasury, was the guest of Rudolph A. Peterson, president of the Bank of America. J. George Harrar, president of the Rockefeller Foundation, was the guest of Frederick Seitz, president of Rockefeller University. Admiral Thomas H. Moorer, chairman of the Joint Chiefs of Staff, was the guest of one of his bosses, Deputy Secretary of Defense David Packard (a California multimillionaire in private life). A. Mims Thomason, president of United Press, was the guest of Jack R. Howard, president of Scripps-Howard Newspapers.

Nor are the several father-son teams surprising. For example, Edgar F. Kaiser of Kaiser Industries brought Edgar F. Kaiser, Jr.; Henry S. Morgan of the preeminent investment banking house of Morgan Stanley & Co., invited Charles F. Morgan; William A. Patterson of United Air Lines, hosted William A. Patterson, Jr.; and Frederic H. Brandi of the investment banking firm of Dillon, Read brought James H. Brandi.

More intriguing are several of the government-business pairings. Paul Rand Dixon, chairman of the Federal Trade Commission, was the guest of oil man and Democratic fat cat Edwin W. Pauley. John D. Ehrlichman, until recently right-hand man to President Nixon, was the guest of Republican fat cat Leonard Firestone. Walter J. Hickel, Secretary of the Interior at the time, and deeply involved in negotiations concerning the Santa Barbara oil spill, was the guest of Fred L. Hartley, president of Union Oil, the company responsible for said oil spill.

The club's board of directors has the right as a group to invite guests. Many of their guests were people in public life: Joseph Alioto, Mayor of San Francisco; Melvin Laird, Secretary of Defense; Alfred Nelder, Chief of Police in San Francisco; Peter J. Pitchess, Sheriff of Los Angeles County; Samuel Yorty, Mayor of Los Angeles; and Ronald Reagan, Governor of California. (Governor Reagan, a frequent guest at the Grove in recent years, used the occasion of the 1967 encampment for an off-the-record meeting with Richard M. Nixon, at which a political compromise was reached in regard to the race for the Republican presidential nomination: "In a private meeting at Bohemian Grove, in July of 1967, Reagan said he would step in only if Nixon faltered.")[15]

It is also interesting to look at the guests in terms of camps. Mandalay, already laden with some of the biggest names in corporate America, included among its guests Peter M. Flanigan, a partner in the investment banking house of Dillon, Read (then serving as a White House aide for foreign trade); John D. Ehrlichman; Thomas S. Gates, Jr., chairman of Morgan Guaranty Trust Bank; Amory Houghton, former chairman of Corning Glass Works; Henry Kearns, chairman of the Export-Import Bank in Washington, D.C.; David M. Kennedy, Secretary of the Treasury; Walter A. Marting, president of Hanna Mining Company; John G. McLean, president of Continental Oil Company; Andrew G. C. Sage, a general partner in the investment banking firm of Lehman Brothers; and Dorrance

15. Gary Wills, *Nixon Agonistes* (Boston: Houghton Mifflin, 1970), p. 256.

Sexton, chairman of Johnson and Higgins, general insurance brokers in New York.

People often ask about the degree of "cohesiveness" and "intimacy" within the higher circles of American business and government. One of the best answers is to be found under the stars in the Bohemian Grove as these men of power camp together in Mandalay, Lost Angels, Cave Man, Midway, Green Mask, Hill Billies, Pink Onion, and Stowaway.

The Bohemian Club

The Bohemian Grove is the property of the Bohemian Club of San Francisco, a club which celebrated its hundredth anniversary in 1972. While the Grove encampment is the club's most famous venture, it is by no means its only activity. The Bohemian Club is a year-round operation of great variety.

The Clubhouse

The Bohemian "clubhouse" is an imposing six-story building only a few blocks from the financial district of downtown San Francisco. It contains all the amenities of the usual upper-class club, except that it has no athletic facilities whatsoever. For more active pursuits, such as swimming, people have to become members next door at the Olympic Club or over a few blocks at the Pacific Union Club.

The main floor of the clubhouse contains the traditional oversized reading room with large stuffed chairs. The room looks like it was developed from one of the traditional clubman cartoons in *The New Yorker*. It features newspapers and magazines from all over world, little statues on pedestals and tables, high-vaulted ceilings, a plush Oriental rug, and members reading their *Wall Street Journals.* "It's almost like a church in its atmosphere," says one nonbusinessman member. Also on the main floor is an equally large domino room, where men can satisfy their gaming passions at little green tables seating four people. Lunchtime tournaments are held quite regularly. The pride of the main floor, however, is the "cartoon room," an extremely spacious barroom, complete with piano and small stage, and decorated with the paintings, handbills, posters, and cartoons drawn by famous club artists for jinks and testimonial dinners of the past. Dice lie conveniently on the bar itself so gentlemen can indulge their gambling urge as a means of determining who signs the check for the drinks. Just off the cartoon room there is a little art gallery. The small shows in the gallery are changed frequently, and of course feature the work of club members.

One floor above the main one are a very large dining room and a library room. The dining room is used for daily lunches as well as for most of the regular Thursday night club entertainments. On the same floor is a smaller dining room called the Grove Room. Its walls are completely covered with beautiful murals of the center of the Grove. The Grove Room is used for more intimate luncheons and parties.

For extremely large parties, testimonial dinners, and dances, there are a reception room and a banquet room in the basement. These rooms, along with the large art gallery on that floor, are sometimes rented by members for private parties and wedding celebrations. The subbasement of the clubhouse is a large theater (seating capacity, 611) where the biggest performances of the regular year are held. The theater also is in constant use for High Jinks and Low Jinks rehearsals, and for orchestra and band practice. Just behind the theater there is a shop for making stage sets, as well as costume rooms and makeup rooms.

The top two floors of the clubhouse contain small meeting rooms, rehearsal rooms, and several small apartments and rooms which usually are rented to older resident members and out-of-town members temporarily located in San Francisco. There is a glass-covered sun deck on the roof.

Directors and Committees

The Bohemian Club is governed by a fifteen-man board of directors elected from among the regular members by the vote of regular members only. The directors, of course, do very little of the day-to-day work themselves. To carry out their wishes they have a hired manager, who in turn has a large staff of cooks, waiters, carpenters, and laborers.

Like most organizations in the United States, the club is run through a set of semiautonomous committees, and it is the job of the board of directors to appoint these committees. In this case there are such committees as a Jinks Committee to look after shows and plays, a Grove Committee to take care of the maintenance of the Grove, a House and Restaurant Committee to direct the dining facilities, an Art Committee to set up art shows at the clubhouse and the Grove, a Library Committee, and a Membership Committee.

Perhaps the most enjoyable service is on the Wine Committee. It meets about five times a year for "working" sessions. In 1970 the committee savored 35 new wines, accepting only 10 to a club stock that includes about 115 different wines. The committee also makes sure that 3,500 bottles of wine are on hand for purchase by members and guests at the Grove encampment. The head of the committee for years has been Maynard A. Amerine, one of the world's foremost authorities on wines and the wine-making process. He is professor of viticulture and oenology at the University of California, Davis.

The Grove Committee was first formed in 1900 when the club finally purchased the land it had been using for many of its encampments since 1880. At that time the Grove was an undeveloped piece of land of only 160 acres, although another 120 acres was added in the next few years. When a real-estate development was started on nearby land in 1913, the club moved to stop that "threatened encroachment" by buying hundreds and hundreds more acres.[16] Land purchases continued throughout the decades, and the Grove reached its present size of 2,700 acres in 1944. The Grove Committee has to oversee the maintenance of the many buildings which have been added since the beautifully architected Grove Clubhouse overlooking the river, the first permanent structure, was erected in 1904. Additionally, there is a parking lot which must be continually enlarged, wells that have to be deepened, and a dispensary that has to have medical supplies (370 people checked into the dispensary in 1970; two people died, one at the Grove, one in an ambulance on the way to San Francisco). The committee also has to have the Grove ready for such activities as the Spring Jinks (a weekend of entertainment), the June Picnic (when members bring their wives to the Grove for a Saturday afternoon), and private parties by members. Nearly 7,000 peo-

16. *Bohemian Club,* San Francisco, 1969, p. 24. This is the handbook for individual members, containing officers and directors, constitution, bylaws, house rules, a list of deceased members, and a brief history of the club.

ple visit the Grove between encampments for one occasion or another.

The Jinks Committee and the House and Restaurant Committee have a common concern: encouraging a large enough attendance at luncheons and entertainments to pay the financial bills. With costs going up all the time, there is a fear that club operations will slip into the red. "To put it simply, we need more people using the club at lunch time," says the 1969–70 report of the House and Restaurant Committee. "Our luncheon business has dropped off for many reasons, and great effort will be put forth in the future by the new committee, we trust, to induce the membership to come to lunch at the club more often."[17] Recently, economies had to be introduced into the food service, and there was a restructuring of prices, dues, and fees.

The Jinks Committee constantly worries over attendance at the programs it puts on at the downtown clubhouse during the year. "They have to reach a minimum attendance or they're in trouble," says my informant close to Jinks operations. "The question always is—will a given play or show draw well? Will four hundred or so people show up for dinner and drinks?" In short, the Bohemian Club is a large enough institution to have needs of its own. Leaders have to devise ways of tempting members to come to the club more often—so that the needs of the institution can be met. The club no longer merely serves the needs of its members. Now the members must serve the needs of the club. "There could be major changes in the structure of the club within the next few years," says one knowledgeable

17. *Report of the President and the Treasurer*, 1969–70, p. 23. This document is available at the California Historical Society in San Francisco.

observer. "Maybe it has become too big and too expensive, and will have to become a more conventional rich man's club."

Becoming a Member

The Membership Committee is the major gatekeeper of the Bohemian Club, for membership is of course by invitation only. A potential member must be nominated by at least two regular members of the club who will vouch for his character and describe the qualities that will make him a "good Bohemian." (However, honorary associates are allowed to sponsor applicants for associate membership.) The prospect himself must fill out a membership application form obtained for him by his sponsors. The form requests the usual information necessary on any application for credit or a license, along with such tidbits as wife's maiden name, business or professional connections, other club memberships, and the names of five people in the club who know him. The hopeful candidate then returns this membership application to his first sponsor, who fills out a part of it which asks for information on "musical, oratorical, literary, artistic, or histrionic talents," as well as for the names of three members of the club who are known by the sponsor to be well acquainted with the applicant. Next the form goes to the second sponsor, who answers the same questions as the first sponsor in addition to listing five members of the club to whom the applicant is personally known.

The prospect then makes appointments to see individually the members of the Membership Committee. He goes by their places of business or law to be asked questions about why he wants to become a member of the Bohemian Club, but even more to be lectured by them about what it means to be a "good Bohemian."

In the meantime, the Membership Committee has been soliciting letters of recommendation about the candidate from some or all of the club members suggested by the candidate and his sponsors as people who know him well. The committee also circulates a monthly notice to all club members, listing people being considered for membership and asking for any opinions (positive or negative) anyone might have on any of the people listed. The notice lists the person's name, age, occupation, and sponsors. Finally, after this rigorous screening, there is the vote. Nine of the eleven members of the Membership Committee have to favor the candidate before he can become a member. Three negative votes and he has to wait at least three years before being proposed again.

Gaining the necessary votes does not make a person automatically a member, however, for there is a long waiting list. Over eight hundred people are backed up to become regular resident members; over six hundred are on the nonresident waiting list. I talked to one regular member who had been on the waiting list for over ten years before becoming a member.

New associate members have no trouble claiming their rightful place—there are no waiting lists for men of talent. "And if you are 'Jinks material,' which means you'll write or perform in Grove plays and shows, then they'll zip you right through," says one informant familiar with Jinks operations. It is not surprising that the club constantly searches for Jinks material. The talented members not only have the two-week encampment to plan for, but they must put on some kind of performance every Thursday night from October to May. "Over the years," says the club handbook, "the demands on the talented members of the Club have increased tremendously with three major productions and twelve Campfire or related programs during the Encampment and twenty or more Thursday nights in the City Club with five or six of these listed as major events."[18]

Even this brief overview of the club and its activities makes clear that it is a twenty-four-hour-a-day, twelve-month-of-the-year operation. As a recent president used to say in his letter of congratulations to new members, "You have joined not only a club, but a way of life."

Carrying a Spear in Bohemia

The Membership Committee is concerned to elect only "good Bohemians," and men often talk about whether or not a fellow member is a "good Bohemian." What does such a phrase mean? A good Bohemian is first of all one who "participates." He acts in shows, he writes poetry, or he tells good after-dinner stories. Even if he doesn't have anything in the way of talent, he still can be a good Bohemian if he faithfully attends and actively enjoys the various performances. Stress must be put on "actively enjoys" because the great scourge of Bohemia is the member who sits back passively and wants to be mindlessly entertained without having to make any mental effort to "appreciate" what is going on around him. "Participation and appreciation are the cornerstones of Bohemia"—so say the opening lines of the members' handbook.

The associates, needless to say, have to be good Bohemians. They are on a year-to-year basis and are spared the $2,000

18. *Bohemian Club* (San Francisco, 1969), p. 27.

initiation fee and $36 basic monthly dues precisely because they are expected to perform. Among regular members, becoming a good Bohemian is an ideal many wish they had the time and talent to attain, but only a minority reach it. This minority is highly esteemed within the club. They are liked by the associate members for their talent and energy, and looked on as a source of pride by the other regular members. "Look," the less-active regular members seem to be saying, "we regular members contribute to Bohemia too."

Less-talented regular members can be Bohemians in good standing if they will "carry a spear for Bohemia," which means they are willing to pitch in when needed—to do little walk-on parts in plays, to paint scenery, or to move pianos around the stage. In this spirit, some very prominent people become mere spear carriers within the Bohemian Club. Edgar F. Kaiser, chairman of Kaiser Industries, was an acolyte in the Cremation of Care in 1969. Louis Niggeman, president of the Fireman's Fund Insurance Company, was a fire bearer in the same ceremony in 1972. Leland I. Doan of the Dow Chemical Company family was one of three men in a group walk-on part in the 1969 High Jinks. DeWitt Peterkin, Jr., vice chairman of Morgan Guaranty Trust Bank, was one of fifteen "male villagers" milling around on stage in scenes of the same play. Wayne E. Thompson, senior vice-president of Dayton-Hudson Department Stores, did Peterkin one better: he was one of eight female villagers who provided backdrop for the main actors.

Other famous people are found working as stagehands or ushers. "Once he was stagehand for the club's annual theatrical production," says the *New York Times's* report on Nelson Rockefeller's 1963 visit to the Bohemian Grove to give a Lakeside Talk. "That time he worked with Henry Ford II shifting scenery."[19] For the Little Friday Night and Big Saturday Night shows, minor jobs are routine events for members of the corporate elite young enough to lend a helping hand. Lesser members get a chuckle out of these occasions. "Did you see who's pushing the piano around the stage tonight?" one will say to the other. "Guess who they've got carrying scenery?" another will ask.

The Spirit of Bohemia

Originally, being a good Bohemian was supposed to require even more than participation and appreciation. It was having the carefree, unconventional spirit of the vagabond or struggling artist. It was a way of "being." Specifically, it was being like the mythical "Bohemian" artist celebrated in American letters since the middle of the nineteenth century. Indeed, the origins of the Bohemian Club can be traced directly to this romantic literary and cultural current, for the club's founders were much taken with its major figures and their writings.

"Bohemian," as the name for the unkempt, half-starving artist who is creative in spite of his dire circumstances, comes from the centuries-old French folk belief that European gypsies were originally from the country of Bohemia. American artists searching for a life style picked up the term while lounging in the Paris cafés of the 1850s. They returned to the United States to paint a picture of Parisian Bohemianism which has made the artists' colony there the envy of American artists and uni-

19. Wallace Turner, "Rockefeller Faces Scrutiny of Top Californians: Governor to Spend Weekend at Bohemian Grove among State's Establishment" (*New York Times*, July 26, 1963), p. 30.

versity students ever since. They also set up their own Bohemia in New York, writing poetry and novels, painting, and engaging in literary criticism.

Romantic spirits around the country became enamored of these New York Bohemians. Journalists, authors, and artists in San Francisco were no exception, and in 1872 they joined together to embody their carefree fantasies and creative urges in the Bohemian Club. It was to be a club for "the promotion of social and intellectual intercourse between journalists and other writers, artists, actors and musicians, professional or amateur, and such others not included in this list as may by reason of knowledge and appreciation of polite literature and the fine arts be deemed worthy of membership."[20] By these criteria, businessmen, lawyers, and other worldly types were to be admitted only if they had special knowledge or appreciation of the arts.

The Bohemian Club struggled mightily to establish its ties with "real Bohemianism." Ambrose Bierce, later to be one of the fathers of West Coast Bohemianism, and the author of such scary semiclassics as *The Devil's Dictionary*, was an early member. So was poet Charles Warren Stoddard, who in 1876 had gained great notoriety by accompanying New York's so-called Queen of Bohemia, Ada Clare, on a sightseeing trip in Hawaii. Bret Harte and Mark Twain were made honorary members. George Sterling, a prosperous real-estate man who became one of the leaders of Western Bohemianism when he turned to poetry, joined the club in 1904. Even socialist author Jack London, who resisted the label of Bohemian for that of vagabond, was acceptable for membership at the turn of the century, although there was some concern expressed over his

20. Fletcher, *The Annals of the Bohemian Club*, Vol. I, pp. 26–27.

radical ideas and his fancy white silk shirts with long, flowing ties.[21]

Alas, despite the high hopes of the San Francisco admirers of "real Bohemians" who first dreamed up the Bohemian Club, the Bohemian spirit had to be compromised from the first. "The members were nearly all impecunious," wrote a not-so-impecunious charter member, Edward Bosqui, in his late-nineteenth-century diary, "and there was much difficulty in devising means to furnish the rooms and to defray current expenses. It was soon apparent," continued Bosqui, "that the possession of talent, without money, would not support the club; and at a meeting of the board of directors [here ten names are listed] it was decided that we should invite an element to join the club which the majority of the members held in contempt, namely men who had money as well as brains, but who were not, strictly speaking, Bohemians. As soon as we began to act upon this determination the problem of our permanent success was solved."[22]

So the calculating rationality of the marketplace had to be part of the club's ethos almost from its founding, and some of the richest men in San Francisco were soon enjoying membership. The club became known as a socially elite organization. While not considered as high status as the Pacific Union Club, it was listed in the *Elite Directory* (1879), the *San Francisco Blue Book* (1888), *Our Society Blue Book* (1894–95), and other social registers of that era. By 1879 one in every seven members of the very exclusive Pacific Union Club was also a

21. Richard O'Connor, *Jack London: A Biography* (Boston: Little, Brown, 1964), p. 151. London liked the Grove very much and seldom missed an encampment.

22. Edward Bosqui, *Memoirs of Edward Bosqui* (Oakland: Holmes Book Company, 1952), pp. 126–127.

member of the Bohemian Club, with the figure climbing to one in five by 1894 and one in four by 1906. In 1907, the first year for which the California Historical Society in San Francisco has copies of the yearly San Francisco *Social Register* that is still in use today, 31 percent of the regular local Bohemian Club members were listed in its pages.

Solving the financial problems of the club had its price, of course. In 1880, only eight years after its founding, a group of painters and writers protested that "the present day is not as the past days, the salt has been washed out of the Club by commercialism, the chairs are too easy and the food too dainty, and the true Bohemian spirit has departed."[23] Around the turn of the century one early member anonymously decried this change in spirit in a little booklet on "Early Bohemia." "The entering of the money-social element has not benefited the Club, as a Bohemian Club," he claimed. Now the club had "social aspirations which means death to genius and a general dead-level mediocrity." Elsewhere he noted, "In the beginning, rich men were absolutely barred, unless they had something of the elements of true Bohemianism (could do something). . . . Now they get in *because* they are rich."[24]

The tension which sometimes flared between the rich and the talented members also was experienced by the most famous artist member of the 1880s, Jules Tavernier. Tavernier became so annoyed at one point that he drew an extra cartoon for a Jinks night, which he displayed in the clubhouse without the permission of the Jinks Committee. "It was an allegorical car-

23. Albert Parry, *Garrets and Pretenders: A History of Bohemianism in America* (New York: Dover Publications, 1933, 1960), p. 226.

24. *Early Bohemia* (no author, no date), pp. 4–5. This small, privately printed book is available in the California Historical Society in San Francisco.

toon," reminisced a long-time member in 1907, "the artist's idea being: Bohemia is fallen into the hands of the Bourgeois—weaving spiders have spun their nets over Bohemia's halls—the Owl has taken flight from Bohemia. In effect, the cartoon represented a Bohemia where trade and barter were followed, and where there were money changers, as in the temple." This unexpected addition to the evening's entertainment greatly offended many wealthy members, which is said to have pleased Tavernier greatly. Usually the cartoons painted by artist members were hung on the walls, but Tavernier took this one away at the end of the evening, proudly announcing that it was "too good for the Bourgeois."[25]

Thus, by the time George Sterling wrote his 1907 Grove play, *The Triumph of Bohemia,* in which the spirit of Bohemia triumphed over the spirit of Mammon, the opposite had long since occurred within the halls of the Bohemian Club. "[Sterling hadn't] noticed," says Albert Parry, a somewhat cynical student of the history of American Bohemianism, "that [the] happy sprites and Bacchic fauns whom he so proudly commanded in his onslaught of Mammon were in reality fat businessmen of San Francisco out on a summer picnic, ready to be amused and flattered by Sterling's plays."[26]

In 1927, when the club excluded modern art from its annual art exhibit because it was "in radical and unreasonable departure from laws of art," there was hardly a stir, although a few artist members threatened to resign and start a new club under

25. Jerome A. Hart, "Tavernier, Artiste-Peintre," March 2, 1907. In "Oversized San Francisco Miscellaneous, Bohemian Club," California Historical Society, San Francisco.
26. Parry, *Garrets and Pretenders,* pp. 238–39. Sterling was given a free room in the club. He lived there from the early 1900s until he died by his own hand in 1926.

a "no censorship" banner. People by then expected that the president of the highly respectable Bohemian Club would say, "The line must be drawn somewhere between what is and what is not art."[27] Nor was it shocking a year later when the club changed its mind about membership for the great comedian Will Rogers because (1) he stole the show at the Grove and (2) told a reporter the encampment was "a form of week-end divertissement for tired business men from which it took them about two weeks to recover."[28] This latter remark was clearly gossip unbecoming a gentleman. Besides, Rogers's remarks were thought by some to be harmful to the candidacy of that swinging Bohemian, Herbert C. Hoover, who was running for the presidency on a "dry" platform.

Unconventionality and a devil-may-care attitude, then, are not the spirit of the Bohemian Club. Avant-garde artists and authors like Jules Tavernier and Jack London are no longer welcome even as guests at the Bohemian Grove. Art Linkletter, Bing Crosby, Ray Bolger, Herman Wouk, and George Shearing are more typical of the artists and authors invited to mingle with the anointed. The real spirit of this Bohemia is a *quid pro quo* arrangement between the rich and the talented. The rich patrons, through their wealth, provide a setting within which the creative members can exercise their talents and enjoy the amenities of a first-rate men's club. Then too, the artists can find customers for their paintings, performers can make connections that lead to engagements at private parties and other social events, and professors can cultivate financial backing for

27. "Bohemians Torn Over Art" (*New York Times,* February 20, 1927), Section II, p. 4.
28. "Won't Name Will Rogers: Bohemian Club Sponsor Quits, San Francisco Paper Says" (*New York Times,* November 23, 1928), p. 22.

their new projects. In return for their patronage, the wealthy are handsomely entertained by the talented members at the Grove and the clubhouse. They also have the privilege of rubbing shoulders with people of very different abilities from their own, which enhances both their self-image and their public image. Some even develop fast friendships with the artistic and professorial members, friendships they never would have developed if the Bohemian Club and its Grove hadn't provided an institutional setting in which the rich and the talented were able to interact on a cooperative and fraternal basis.

The way in which the club aids talented members is nicely documented in the case of Professor Ernest O. Lawrence, the Berkeley physicist who developed the cyclotron so important in the early phases of atomic and nuclear research. Lawrence's work in the 1930s was supported financially by the university and foundations, but he needed even more funds to develop a larger cyclotron:

> [Lawrence] had got all he could hope for from the University budget, but he saw an untapped spring in the Regents personally. Most of them belonged to an Elk's Club of the very rich called the Bohemian, which maintained a wonderful rustic lodge on the Russian River fifty miles north of Berkeley. . . . Invitations were coveted; there was no more intoxicating distinction than to wash dishes at the Bohemian Grove while President [Robert G.] Sproul [of the University of California] dried them. Sproul supported Lawrence as faithfully at the Grove as at board meetings. He helped Lawrence to a jovial kitchen-sink intimacy with two of the most influential Regents, John Neylan and William Crocker.[29]

29. Nuel Pharr Davis, *Lawrence and Oppenheimer* (New York: Simon and Schuster, 1968), pp. 69–70. In 1942 the Bohemian Grove was the site

As a result of this kitchen-sink intimacy, Neylan made himself the chairman of a special regents' subcommittee to look after the needs of Lawrence's radiation laboratory. Crocker, chairman of the university regents, gave Lawrence $75,000 in 1937 for a new building to house the bigger cyclotron.

The arrangement between the rich and the talented, then, is advantageous to members of both groups; each gets something it wouldn't otherwise have. The anonymous author of *Early Bohemia* comprehended some of the mutual benefits in his turn-of-the-century complaint:

> Things have changed; now the simply rich become members because it is fashionable to say, "I am a member of the Bohemian Club," and they imagine that some of the reputed brightness of the Club will be reflected on them. The poor artist or literary man gets in, by hook or by crook, because he thinks he may be able to sell some of his brains to the merely rich. So both are satisfied, in a way; but neither wholly.[30]

The Bohemian Club, bringing together as it does the wealthy and the talented, is an unusual club. However, the Bohemian Grove, with its two-week retreat for a nationwide clientele, is not only unusual but utterly unique within the American upper class. Given the Grove's great success, it is not surprising that it has had some imitators, and it is to those imitators that we now turn.

---

at which leaders of the atomic-bomb project decided which experimental nuclear plants to build in their search for a usable atomic weapon. I am grateful to John Van der Zee, author of *Power at Ease: Inside the Greatest Men's Party on Earth* (New York: Harcourt Brace Jovanovich, 1974), for calling this reference to my attention.

30. *Early Bohemia*, p. 5.

2

Other Watering Holes

John J. Mitchell of Chicago and Santa Barbara, now in his seventy-sixth year, is a prototypical member of the American upper class. Born into a wealthy Illinois family (his father was president of a large Chicago bank), John went to school at the Hill School in Pennsylvania, one of the top Eastern boarding schools for boys, and Yale University.

Leaving Yale during World War I, he joined the Naval Aviation Service. Due to a serious injury in an airplane crash, he had to withdraw from the military. After a long recovery from this near tragedy he became, in 1920, a clerk in his father's bank. By 1927 he was an assistant to the vice president. Mitchell might have continued to move up the bank hierarchy, but in 1921 he married Lolita Armour of the meat-packing family. Thus, the pull was strong to join an Armour enterprise. In 1931 he became vice president and treasurer of Universal Oil Products, which Lolita had inherited from her father.

Like so many men of his social class, Mitchell was a member of gentlemen's clubs. His first club was the exclusive Chicago Club. However, through numerous visits to California, he also knew people in the Bohemian Club of San Francisco, and in 1928 he became a member. Mitchell was especially taken by the Bohemian Grove encampment. The idea of a friendly, re-laxed get-together in a beautiful setting seemed worthy of imitation: "Impressed by the combination of friendship and forest trees, Jack asked himself: 'Why don't we use the themes of fellowship, a lovely country and a lovely time of the year down in Santa Barbara County, but make the horse the central motif of it?' "[1]

Mitchell tried his idea on some friends in the Santa Barbara area. Coincidentally, they had been thinking of something very similar, a ride that would last over a period of several days. So, a few months later, Mitchell purchased a 6,500-acre ranch about forty miles from the city of Santa Barbara. It was to be the home base for the southern California version of the Bohe-mian Grove.

In April, 1930, Mitchell gathered sixty-five men on his ranch for an overnight ride. This trial run was enthusiastically ap-plauded, and plans were made for a longer ride a month later. Moreover, a prominent rancher came up with a name for the group, Rancheros Visitadores (Visiting Ranchers). The name Rancheros Visitadores gave Mitchell the tie to California tradi-tion he had been groping for. The week would be organized to commemorate a traditional ride from the days when ranch-ers and Spanish missions were the dominant features of the southern California landscape. Mitchell and his friends focused on the years between 1770 and 1860, the years when the ranchers would join together to drive their cattle to the nearest mission, there to be met by another group of ranchers, who would take the combined herds on to the next mission (and so on until the cattle reached market). According to legend,

1. Neill C. Wilson, *Los Rancheros Visitadores: Twenty-Fifth Anniver-sary* (Rancheros Visitadores, 1955), pp. 17–18.

the men, once relieved of their herds, would have a rip-snorting good time on their carefree trip back to their own ranches.

It was the return rides of the old rancheros that John J. Mitchell decided to make the historical precedent for his new social occasion. He would invite people to his ranch for a week-long ride through southern California ranch land. There would be good food, lively entertainment, and rodeo contests. It was not quite the Bohemian Grove in all its details, but it was pretty close in its goals and format.

Rancho Juan y Lolita, as Mitchell called his new home, had to become a setting worthy of a riding group pretending to the traditions of the Rancheros Visitadores. Mitchell therefore dispatched his personal secretary, Elmer Awl, to search out and purchase available memorabilia of early California that would provide the proper flavor and a ring of authenticity for the new group. Within a few years the RVs, as they called themselves for short, were to own innumerable stagecoaches, wagons, surreys, buckboards, rigs, saddles, and other artifacts of the mission days. Many of the smaller purchases were displayed in a Barbary Coast saloon which Mitchell constructed in a barn on his property. The pride of this structure was an elegant mahogany bar that Mitchell and Awl rescued from a storage company. It had been made for a famous saloon which once enlivened the center of nineteenth-century Santa Barbara.[2]

Mitchell also decided to import some unusual wildlife even though it was not part of the mission-days motif. Along with 450 head of cattle and 125 horses, he stocked his land with 3 kangaroos, 10 sacred cattle from India, 15 Belgian draft horses,

2. Thomas F. Collison, *El Diario del Viaje de los Rancheros Visitadores* (Santa Barbara *News-Press*, 1935), p. 106.

10 Sicilian donkeys, and 3 buffaloes. Here, truly, was a grazing area that would be of interest to even the most jaded of week-end cowboys.

Ninety men joined the first Ranchero ride in May, 1930. They responded to an invitation which advised, among other things, that "purely western costume of the days of 50 years ago should be worn."[3] (This emphasis on old-fashioned attire caught on quickly, and today many members have elaborate cowboy costumes, as well as elegant silver saddles for their horses.) This initial trek, lasting four days, began on rancher Dwight Murphy's vast acreage and moved on for a two-day stay at the Rancho Juan y Lolita. An amateur rodeo contest was held on the third day. The fourth morning was highlighted by a visit to nearby Mission Santa Ines, about five miles from the Juan y Lolita, a visit which was to become a regular part of the ride. Most of those pioneer riders were Santa Barbara ranchers and businessmen.

The first ride, predictably enough, was judged a big success, and the RVs grew steadily in numbers. There were a hundred riders in 1931, 135 in 1932. By 1939, the first year there was a seven-day program, the membership had doubled to 200 and most of the events had acquired the forms which persist to this day, when over 750 members and guests (along with a supporting cast of about 300 hired hands) gather on the first Saturday in May.

The exact route of the ride has been altered slightly over the years, partly to make way for the real-estate developers, partly to make the ride shorter and less onerous for the aging

3. *Historia de los Rancheros Visitadores* (Santa Barbara *News-Press*, 1939), p. 11.

membership. (Riders used to be in the saddle, or on the buckboard, for ninety miles; now the distance is more likely to be forty to sixty miles.) For many years the RVs assembled on ranch lands near Santa Barbara, then rode four miles to the Mission Santa Barbara for a blessing by the mission padres. Now that particular Ranchero camp is a city park, and the RVs receive the necessary blessing at the more rural Santa Ines Mission about forty miles northeast of the city. The trip to the Santa Ines Mission has become an elaborate ceremonial occasion. The little tourist-trap town of Solvang, on whose outskirts the mission is located, has incorporated the Ranchero Visitadores folderol as one of its historic "attractions." Two sociology students who witnessed the 1973 proceedings summarized the event as follows:

Saturday afternoon was the traditional public ceremony in which padres at the Santa Ines Mission bless the Rancheros and their mounts. Gaping crowds lined the streets as the 700 Rancheros rode double-file through the main street of Solvang and gathered at the mission. A creaky opera-style baritone crooned the Ranchero theme song as the RV and California flags fluttered side by side in the breeze. The padre's blessing was followed by the "Empty Saddles" ceremony held in honor of the members who had died during the year. The mission bells tolled and the horse, carrying the symbolic "empty saddle," whinnied mournfully as the names of the dead were called out.

But the solemnity was soon over as the Rancheros split gleefully for the nearest bar. This was the big moment for the local children, who each year clamor for the "privilege" of holding the horses while the Rancheros are in the bars. The children receive tips for this service, and according to one enterprising boy who was holding two horses, "the drunker the guy, the bigger the tip."[4]

The Rancheros' week together is a busy one, which includes much more than riding. Early in the week there is a horse show one day and horse races the next, featuring some of the finest and most expensive horses in California. Both events are held on a track built by the club on the ten-thousand-acre Alisal Guest Ranch. Later in the week there is a rodeo featuring both imported professional talent and amateur events for the members. This event used to take place on the Juan y Lolita, but now it is held at the RVs San Marcos Camp, where a special arena has been built, complete with holding pens, chutes, and bleacher seats.

Rodeo star Montie Montana is chairman of the RV rodeo committee, which ensures the club the best rodeo performers in the country as guest stars year after year. The rodeo activities are announced by real-estate developer Frank M. Bogert, former Mayor of Palm Springs. Bogert maintains a steady drumfire of sarcasm and humor which the members find hilarious. "It all proves anyone can beat a Texan," he will say if the loser in an event happens to be from Texas. Another one of his lines: "A Texan would stick a knife in your back—then have you arrested for carrying a concealed weapon."[5]

Rancheros whose riding skills are not of the highest caliber are encouraged to participate in such relatively easy and comedylike events as calf roping, mule racing, calf ribbon-

4. Peggy Rodgers and Donna Beck, "The Rancheros Visitadores," Unpublished paper, 1973.
5. Barney Brantingham, "Rancheros Hit Trail Again Today" (Santa Barbara News-Press, May 9, 1966), p. B–1. Nineteen-sixty-six was the last year the News-Press gave detailed coverage to the ride.

65

tying, yokel cow milking, greenhorn sack roping, and musical chairs on horseback. In some years the participants fill out an application form which reads in part as follows:

> I offer myself herewith, in all my obnoxiousness, as a sacrifice on the altar of Ranchero entertainment. . . . This is entirely my own idea—nobody wants me in the damn thing, so just to be ornery, to enjoy myself and to disgust everyone, I herewith forcefully enter myself in the events checked. . . .[6]

Despite such ominous application forms, as many as seventy-five to one hundred members and guests sometimes participate in the rodeo.

There is other daytime entertainment for the many hours when the members are not riding. Skeet shooting and trap shooting are regular features; so are various horsemanship contests and swimming.

There is also evening entertainment. The silver-anniversary history published by the club speaks of high jinks and low jinks, but the programs are not nearly as large or as organized as those put on at the Bohemian Grove. Few club members participate. Instead, famous entertainers like Phil Harris and Jim Nabors—the featured guests of 1973—join with lesser-known talents such as the RVs' fifteen-piece Western band on the RV stage. Down through the years Rancheros could boast of such guests as Billy O'Neill, Ken Maynard, The King's Men, Clark Gable, Roy Rogers, Gene Autry, Kay Kayser, and Bob Hope. And Edgar Bergen and Art Linkletter, old standbys of the Bohemian Grove, liked the Rancheros so much that they became members of this club too.

6. Wilson, *Rancheros Visitadores: Twenty-Fifth Anniversary,* p. 84.

Unlike the Bohemian Club, famous academics and artists are not a prominent feature of the Ranchero landscape. Nonetheless, the club can count as members and guests a *Who's Who* of those who became known for their paintings of cowboy and Western scenes: Frank Tenney Johnson, Ed Borein, Joe De Yong, Nicholas S. Firfires, Will James, Clyde Forsythe, Channing Peake, and Bill Woggon. During the rides such artist members contribute sketches, portraits, and cartoons to the festivities. By far the most famous RV artist member was the late Walt Disney, known for cartoons and movies rather than Western paintings. Disney's drawings for the club of Donald Duck in a sombrero marked with the RV brand, or Mickey Mouse swinging a Ranchero lariat, brought special pleasure to the members.

Two evenings of the trek are taken up with initiation-type ceremonies. On the opening night, first-time riders are put through a mild hazing, which includes both serious and inane questions about horses and horsemanship. On the second night new members—those who have ridden for at least three out of the previous five years and been found acceptable by the membership committee—are treated to a welcoming ceremony. Then they are allowed to display proudly the official RV emblem, which was designed in 1931 by a Western artist of the era.

In addition to the opening-night hazing, first-time riders must travel as a group for the first several days as part of "Maverick Camp." This camp serves as an initiation into the Rancheros, for its leader is responsible for indoctrinating the newcomers into RV lore. Mavericks continue to receive prankish harassment during this time, reminiscent of the hazing to which college freshmen or fraternity pledges are sometimes subjected. Mavericks are expected to fight back when hassled by a member, and the interchanges with the new recruits become a part of the general horseplay that characterizes an RV ride. Later in the week the first-timers are permitted to join the camp to which they were originally invited, but not before they have taken part in the chase of greased pigs as their final ordeal.

Evenings are not restricted to entertainment and ceremonies. They also are a time for practical jokes. Since the name of the game for the Rancheros is to "go cowboy" for a week, the fun is much more rough and boisterous than at the more sedate Bohemian Grove, where music and theater are the dominant themes. An RV member is liable to awaken to find his boots nailed to a tree stump. If not nailed down, they may be full of stale beer or urine. His bedroll may be missing when he turns in at night. His saddle may be loosened so he will fall to the ground as he crawls onto his horse. Firecrackers at all hours and in unlikely places were quite the thing for several years. Tents often are cut down in the middle of the night. Sometimes whole camps get leveled. One year a little wooden bridge leading across a stream to one of the camps was completely burned.

As at the Bohemian Grove, great quantities of beer and alcohol help to ease the men into joyous celebration. Some nights it is risky to drink too much, however, for several hours in the saddle loom the next day. Fortunately, there are many surreys, stagecoaches, beer wagons, chuck wagons, and buckboards which can be used by those who party too far into the night. For those who got out of line in their drinking or prankishness, there used to be a mule-drawn jail wagon sometimes called the mobile hoosegow or rolling *calabozo*. This penalty box also was used for those who were "sleeping too soft," which means they had sneaked away from camp for a soft bed in

Solvang or on Alisal Guest Ranch. In recent years, however, the jail wagon has been left behind because it cannot withstand the steep climbs on a newly adopted route.

The roughness of the fun on the RV ride also shows up at the rodeo. One year a guest from Texas fell off his horse and broke his collarbone. Another year a rancher from New Mexico was injured in a fall and a colonel from nearby Vandenburg Air Force Base received a fractured jaw which required surgery. The presence or absence of injuries during a trek is a regular feature of reports on the Rancheros in the local newspaper.

Not all the fun is rough or silly, however. As at the Bohemian Grove, there is a small portion of the membership that slips off the reservation to avail itself of the fifteen to twenty prostitutes who are brought into the area for Ranchero week. A knowledgeable informant explained, "The girls come in each year from Las Vegas and Los Angeles, usually in groups of three to five. Oftentimes," he continued, "you will see some of the same girls for three or four years in a row, maybe even longer. They are brought in by two or three members who have businesses that bring them in contact with such women. One of the guys brings them, I think, because he likes to think of himself as a big wheel—it's a way of showing off. The other guy I know of is more quiet about it—he probably does it because he knows a few of the members like to visit prostitutes."

Arrangements with the prostitutes are consummated in inns and motels around the Solvang area. In times past, the women went to one specific hotel in Santa Barbara at the behest of the hotel's owner, a longstanding RV member. A whole floor was set aside for their activities during the week. "But he's dead now," said our informant, referring to the hotel owner, "and besides, no part of the ride brings the RVs close to Santa Barbara like it used to be."

Since the postwar years, when the club burgeoned in size, the members have been divided into camps which alternate in their behavior toward each other from gracious hospitality to half-serious rivalry. As with the Bohemian Grove, the camps are a source of considerable entertainment, including a familiar feature of men-only parties, stag movies. Several camps even have pianos which are moved from campsite to campsite during the week. Each night a different camp will throw a huge barbecue for the rest of the club, featuring roast pigs, goats, bulls' heads, and other delicacies. Los Borrachos (the drunks) vary the pattern—they have a traditional Tiger's Milk Breakfast at 7 A.M. on Tuesday morning. The breakfast program begins at 6:30 A.M. with the loud music of a band, and features entertainment throughout the meal. Each camp has its own style and nuances, with pretensions of unique horsemanship or riding abilities. Most have private bars and some have special food wagons. Pictures, drawings, and pin-ups decorate the camps, with the Los Borrachos' back-bar mural of an all-female oil-drilling crew being of special interest to newcomers. (The women are nude, of course, except for their hard hats.) The camps even have their own special brands which they put on all of their possessions.[7]

Although Rancheros come from over forty states and Canada to take part in the festivities, the great majority are from California. In 1965, the year for which we were able to obtain one

7. Ibid., p. 81. However, Western affectation is carried to its ultimate limits by the many members who have their own private brands, which they use not only on their horses, but also on their wearing apparel and saddles.

of the guarded membership lists from the friend of a former employee, 74 percent of the 618 regular and honorary members were Californians. The biggest group—189—came from Los Angeles and its suburbs. The Santa Barbara area contributed 82 men, San Francisco was home for 26 members, and 161 people came from the rest of the state.[8] A neighboring Western state, Arizona, provided the biggest out-of-state contingent, 29. Second in importance was Illinois, the original home of club founder John J. Mitchell, with 23. Colorado (11), Nevada (10), New Mexico (8), Oregon (8), New York (7), and Texas (6) are the other states which contributed more than five members.

The Rancheros membership book reveals the occupations of most of the members, making possible a closer look at professional and business connections than in the case of regular members of the Bohemian Club. Just over half of the RVs are businessmen, in occupations ranging from banker to real estate operator. One-fifth of these business members are with companies large enough to be listed in Poor's *Register of Corporations, Executives, and Directors*. The second most important occupational category is that of rancher, with 25 such people from the Santa Barbara area, 84 from the rest of California, and 27 from other states west of the Mississippi (primarily Arizona, New Mexico, Texas, Wyoming, and Montana). The remaining 27 percent of the membership consists of lawyers, physicians, dentists, engineers, architects, retirees, and those who do not state any occupation.

Clearly, then, the Rancheros bring together captains of

8. One-half of the San Francisco members are listed in the San Francisco *Social Register*, 35 percent of the Los Angeles members are in the Los Angeles *Blue Book*, and 18 percent of the Santa Barbara members are in the Los Angeles *Blue Book*.

industry with masters of the land. A common interest in horses and horseplay provides a social setting in which men with different forms of wealth get to know each other better. *Sociologically speaking, the Rancheros Visitadores is an organization which serves the function (whether the originators planned it that way or not) of helping to integrate ranchers and businessmen from different parts of the country into a cohesive social class.*

As might be expected, many of the most prominent members are from out of state, especially as contrasted with the small businessmen and middle-class employees who make up a large part of the Santa Barbara group. For example, Hargrove Bowles, Jr., is a multimillionaire Democrat from Greensboro, North Carolina (he lost a bid for the state governorship in 1972); Randolph Crossley is a major land developer in Hawaii; Brooks McCormick is president of International Harvester in Chicago; John Justin of Fort Worth, Texas, is one of the country's largest boot manufacturers; Rushton Skakel (better known as Ethel Kennedy's brother) is a multimillionaire carbon manufacturer in New York; Philip K. Wrigley is a gum manufacturer of some renown from Chicago; General Frank Schwengel is chairman of the board of Seagram & Sons in New York; and Lucien Wulsin is president of D. H. Baldwin Company (pianos) in Cincinnati. However, the club does not have nearly as many men from big corporations as does its Bohemian counterpart.

The Rancheros boast a rather impressive political roster, headed by California governor Ronald Reagan. Evelle Younger, the Attorney General of California, has been a Ranchero since the mid-fifties, as has Peter Pitchess, the sheriff of Los Angeles County. One California congressman is among the members:

Republican Bob Mathias, a former Olympic decathlon champion. Also on the RV membership list is William P. Clark, Jr., a controversial appointment to the California Supreme Court by Governor Reagan.

As already noted, the Rancheros had to divide into camps because of a postwar increase in membership. There are seventeen camps, sporting such Spanish names as Los Amigos, Los Vigilantes, Los Tontos (bums), Los Bandidos, and Los Flojos (lazy ones). They range in size from fifteen to ninety-three, with the majority of them listing between twenty and sixty members. Most camps have members from a variety of geographical locations, although some are slightly specialized in that regard. Los Gringos, the largest camp, has the greatest number of members from out of state. Los Borrachos, Los Picadores, and Los Chingadores, the next largest camps, have a predominance of people from the Los Angeles area. Los Vigilantes, with twenty members, began as a San Francisco group, but now includes riders from Oregon, Washington, New York, and southern California. Campo Adolfo, the camp to which Governor Reagan and Justice Clark belong, has about forty members. Most are ranchers and land developers from the counties adjoining Santa Barbara, but there are also such out-of-staters as Rushton Skakel, the aforementioned Kennedy in-law, of New York; Thomas A. Reynolds, Jr., a corporation lawyer from Chicago; Haden Upchurch, an oilman from Dallas; and William G. Baker, Jr., an investment banker with Lehman Brothers in New York.

Los Gringos, Los Borrachos, and Los Chingadores are not only three of the largest camps within the Rancheros; they also provide the club with its major linkages to the Bohemian Club. Forty men are members of both clubs—fourteen are Los Chingadores, eight are Los Gringos, and seven are Los Borrachos. Four are in Los Vigilantes, the San Francisco-oriented camp, three are in Los Picadores, another large Los Angeles group, two are in Los Bustardos, one is in Los Vaqueros, and one is in Los Charros.

Some of the most prominent business leaders of California are in this select forty who are both Bohemians and Rancheros. Justin Dart is chairman of Rexall Drug Company and a major Republican financial contributor. Edwin W. Pauley is chairman of Pauley Petroleum, a regent of the University of California, and a major Democratic contributor. Preston Hotchkis of Los Angeles is chairman of Bixby Ranch Company, a large land developer, and a heavy contributor to Republican and anti-conservationist causes. Porter Sesnon of San Francisco is a leading investor in ranch lands and oil. John O'Melveny is the senior partner in Los Angeles' most powerful law firm, O'Melveny and Myers. Lawrence and Melvin Lane are the publishers of *Sunset Magazine*. A complete rundown on the forty interlocking overlappers can be found on pages 76 and 77.

In 1928 the Bohemian Grove provided John J. Mitchell with the inspiration for his retreat on horseback, the Rancheros Visitadores. Since 1930 the RVs have grown to the point where they are an impressive second best to the Grove in size, entertainment, and stature. Their combination of businessmen and ranchers is as unique as the Bohemian's amalgamation of businessmen and artists. It is hardly surprising that wealthy men from Los Angeles, San Francisco, Honolulu, Spokane, and Chicago would join Mitchell in wanting to be members of both.

Roundup Riders of the Rockies

It was May of 1948, and two well-known Colorado gentlemen, businessman Frank H. Ricketson, Jr., and land developer

74

Joe H. Dekker, were flying back to Denver from their annual ride with the Rancheros. They had enjoyed themselves immensely, and their minds continued to dwell on the events of the week. Ricketson, looking out the window at the Rockies far below, remarked, "We have some wonderful country of our own right down there." He had been talking for a long time about doing something to publicize the tourist attractions of the state.

"How better can we advertise the tourist attractions of Colorado than by organizing a horseback ride through the forest near tourist centers?" asked Dekker. Ricketson was right with him: "To accomplish that purpose it will have to be organized by a number of prominent Colorado citizens with the same ideas." "You get the group together," said Dekker, who was well aware of how many prominent citizens Ricketson knew, "and I will organize and plan the details."[9]

And so was born yet another imitator of the Bohemian Grove, directly patterned after the Grove's first imitator. This one was to be called the Roundup Riders of the Rockies (or 3R, as their registered brand would have it). The group was an immediate success and has been riding ever since. In 1972 it celebrated its silver anniversary.

Roundup Riders are not publicity shy. In order to call attention to the glories of Colorado they have sponsored rodeos, parades, television shows, and Western entertainment around the state in addition to allowing themselves to be photographed on ceremonial occasions. In keeping with their interest in tourism, the 100- to 125-mile ride takes a new route each year, thus bringing notice to different areas of the state. Whatever the exact starting point, however, the ride usually begins with a

9. *Tally Book, 1971. Roundup Riders of the Rockies,* p. 98.

Bohemians and Rancheros

NAME	RESIDENCE	OCCUPATION	RV CAMP	BOHEMIAN GROVE CAMP
Willis R. Bailard	Santa Barbara	Rancher	Los Chingadores	Santa Barbara
Edgar Bergen	Los Angeles	Entertainer	Los Picadores	Dragon
Alfred Bone, Jr.	Los Angeles	Airlines executive	Los Bustardos	Spot
Paul M. Browne	San Francisco	Travel-agency owner	Los Chingadores	Owl's Nest
Frank G. Chambers	San Francisco	Venture capitalist	Los Borrachos	Sempervirens
W. Turner Clack	Spokane	Oil producer	Los Vigilantes	Fore Peak
Joseph J. Coney	San Francisco	Rancher, ship owner	Los Vigilantes	Parsonage
Roger A. Converse	Los Angeles	Airlines executive	Los Borrachos	Lost Angels
Hernando Courtright	Beverly Hills	Hotel owner	Los Gringos	Dragon
Randolph A. Crossley	Honolulu	Land developer	Los Gringos	Midway
Justin Dart	Los Angeles	Drugstore chain executive	Los Gringos	Land of Happiness
George A. Ditz	Stockton (Cal.)	Attorney, rancher	Los Chingadores	Sleepy Hollow
John A. Ditz	Stockton (Cal.)	Land developer	Los Chingadores	Hermits
John Flanigan	Los Angeles	Brewery executive	Los Chingadores	Mandalay
John J. Garland	Los Angeles	Realtor	Los Gringos	No camp listed
Preston Hotchkis	Los Angeles	Land developer	Los Chingadores	Lost Angels
John V. Huckins	San Francisco	Hotel owner	Los Vaqueros	Faraway
Charles H. Jackson, Jr.	Santa Barbara	Rancher, land speculator	Los Chingadores	Santa Barbara
George D. Jagels	Los Angeles	Rancher	Los Borrachos	Skiddoo

NAME	RESIDENCE	OCCUPATION	RV CAMP	GROVE CAMP
Ed Le Vesconte	San Bruno (Cal.)	Printer	Los Vigilantes	Fore Peak
Art Linkletter	Los Angeles	Entertainer	Los Picadores	Dragon
Malcolm McDuffie	Los Angeles	Oil executive	Los Borrachos	Lost Angels
John L. Merrill	San Francisco	Rancher, engineer	Los Chingadores	No camp listed
John J. Mitchell	Santa Barbara	Rancher	Los Gringos	Land of Happiness
Arch Monson, Jr.	San Francisco	Electrical wholesaler	Los Vigilantes	Red Fire
Thomas F. Neblett	Los Angeles	Management consultant	Los Bustardos	Wayside Lodge
George J. O'Brien	Los Angeles	Cement executive	Los Chingadores	Lost Angels
John Ohanneson	Alameda (Cal.)	Surgeon	Los Chingadores	Parsonage
John O'Melveny	Los Angeles	Attorney	Los Chingadores	Lost Angels
Edwin W. Pauley	Los Angeles	Oil executive	Los Chingadores	Owl's Nest
Henry Pope, Jr.	Chicago	Hosiery manufacturer	Los Gringos	Land of Happiness
Gallatin Powers	Monterey (Cal.)	Restaurant owner	Los Borrachos	Woof
Carl G. A. Rosen	San Francisco	Consulting engineer	Los Gringos	Edgehill
Porter Sesnon	San Francisco	Rancher, oil land speculator	Los Chingadores	Uplifters
William M. Spencer	Chicago	Transportation executive	Los Gringos	Land of Happiness
Kenneth W. Walters, Jr.	Scottsdale	Rancher, beverage manufacturer	Los Chingadores	Santa Barbara
John S. Wiester	Los Angeles	Insurance broker	Los Charros	Skyhi
Carl Zachrisson	Claremont (Cal.)	Professor	Los Picadores	Fore Peak

public sendoff from a Colorado city amenable to a dose of 3R boosterism, and then heads for the open country, using trails picked with the aid of the Forest Service.

Once on the trail, the concern with the promotion of tourism declines, and the Roundup Riders settle down to socializing and enjoying in proper Bohemian and Ranchero fashion. "The heart of the ride is 20 miles or more a day in the saddle," says Ricketson, "the marvelous scenic area which only a privileged few will enjoy each year, the mountain flowers, the wild game, the bird life."[10]

At night there is entertainment by the 3R's ten-piece band. "We're versatile—country western, Dixieland, symphony—we play 'em all," says entertainment director Pete Smythe, a former Denver radio and television broadcaster. Among the songs in their repertoire is "Come Ride with the Roundup Riders," a song Smythe wrote especially for the group. It concludes with the message that "when you ride with the Roundup Riders Old Mother Nature is thine." Also sure to be played is "Rick, Our King," a tune written by another member in praise of club president "Rick'" Ricketson.

Outside entertainers are brought along on many of the rides. Names from the past who performed for 3R include the late Audie Murphy, Fred MacMurray, Casey Tibbs, Dennis Morgan, and Dale Robertson. Then too, Montie Montana, perennial Ranchero, and other rodeo performers make their appearance in the Roundup Riders' camp.

Nighttime also means practical jokes. One year Joe Dekker and some of his friends brought a pet raccoon and several coon-

10. Robert Pattridge, "Closer to Heaven on Horseback" (*Empire Magazine, Denver Post,* July 9, 1972), for this and following quotes. I am grateful to sociologist Ford Cleere for bringing this article to my attention.

hounds into camp. "We turned the dogs and coon loose when everybody was asleep," Dekker reminisced. "All hell broke loose." Another time Dekker led his forces on an Indian raid: "We went down to one of the Denver stores and rented a dummy and dressed it up like a squaw. We got Montie Montana (the trick roper) and eight or ten others dressed like Indians. They galloped into camp and whooped around the fire until they found the squaw—under Ricketson's bed."

The riders do not carry their fine camp with them. Instead, twenty camphands are employed to move the camp in trucks to the next campsite. Thus, when the Roundup Riders arrive at their destination each evening they find fourteen large sleeping tents complete with cots, air mattresses, portable toilets, and showers. Also up and ready for service are a large green dining tent and an entertainment stage. A diesel-powered generator provides the camp with electricity.

Food service is provided by Martin Jetton of Fort Worth, Texas, a caterer advertised in the southwest as "King of the Barbecue." Breakfasts and dinners are said to be veritable banquets. Lunch is not as elaborate, but it does arrive to the riders on the trail in a rather unusual fashion that only those of the higher circles could afford: "lunches in rugged country are often delivered by light plane or helicopter."[11] One year the men almost missed a meal because a wind came up and scattered the lunches which were being parachuted from two Cessna 170s.

In addition to the twenty hired hands who take care of the camp, there are twenty wranglers to look after the horses. The horses on the ride—predominantly such fine breeds as Arabian,

11. Ibid., p. 12.

Quarter Horse, and Morgan—are estimated to be worth more than $200,000. Horses and riders compete in various contests of skill and horsemanship on a layover day in the middle of the week. Skeet shooting, trap shooting, and horseshoes also are a part of this event.

Membership in the Roundup Riders of the Rockies is limited to 130, considerably less than the Bohemians and Rancheros. The bulk of the membership, as might be expected, is from Colorado. In addition to a solid cross-section of the Denver social and business elite (the biggest names: Charles C. Gates, president of Gates Rubber Company, and John M. King, a financier who donated about $250,000 to the Nixon campaign in 1968), there are thirteen ranchers and numerous medium-sized and small businessmen, hotel owners, and real-estate operators from the rest of the state.

Several veterinarians and physicians also are among the Colorado members. The physicians form a committee which is supposed to be available in case of accidents. Roundup Riders are not as rough as Rancheros, however, and the committee's services have been needed only once. That was in 1963, when a Colorado car dealer and his horse fell off Timberline Trail at the thirteen-thousand-foot level. The man was carried to a hospital by helicopter; he was back in his saddle for the next year's ride.

The forty-five non-Coloradans among the riders come from twenty-two different states, most of them neighbors of Colorado. Although almost all of the out-of-staters are well-to-do businessmen and ranchers, few are of the echelons which congregate at the Bohemian Grove. Burnham Yates is president of the First National Bank in Lincoln, Nebraska; Thomas Frye is president of Idaho First National Bank in Boise; Fred Brown is a top-level executive with United Air Lines; and

Owen C. McEwen is president of Steffen Dairy Foods in Wichita, Kansas. Even more typical are a wholesale distributor in Grand Island, Nebraska; a casket manufacturer in Quincy, Illinois; a rancher in Wyoming; and a savings-bank president from Ann Arbor, Michigan. About one of every five out-of-state businessmen is listed in the Poor's directory, compared to a two out of five figure for out-of-state Ranchero businessmen.

The Roundup Riders, who hold their trek at the same time the Bohemians hold their encampment, must be reckoned as a more regional organization. Although there are numerous millionaires and executives among them, the members are not of the national stature of most Bohemians and many Rancheros. They can afford to invest thousands of dollars in their horses and tack, to pay a $300 yearly ride fee, and to have their lunch brought to them by helicopter, but they cannot compete in business connections and prestige with those who assemble at the Bohemian Grove. Building from the Denver branch of the upper class, the Roundup Riders reach out primarily to Nebraska (six), Texas (five), Illinois (five), Nevada (three), California (three), and Arizona (three). There are no members from New York, Boston, Philadelphia, or other large Eastern cities.

Several other regional rides have been inspired by the Rancheros, rides such as the Desert Caballeros in Wickenburg, Arizona, and the Verde Vaqueros in Scottsdale, Arizona. These groups are similar in size and membership to the Roundup Riders of the Rockies. Like the Roundup Riders, they have a few overlapping members with the Rancheros. But none are of the status of the Rancheros Visitadores. They are minor legacies of the Bohemian Grove, unlikely even to be aware of their kinship ties to the retreat in the redwoods.

3

Do Bohemians, Rancheros, and Roundup Riders Rule America?

The foregoing material on upper-class retreats, which I have presented in as breezy a manner as possible, is relevant to highly emotional questions concerning the distribution of power in modern America. In this final chapter I will switch styles somewhat and discuss these charged questions in a sober, simple, and straightforward way, and I hope I will leave the reader in the end with no doubt that Bohemians, Rancheros, Roundup Riders, and other members of the upper class are the rulers of America.

It is my hypothesis that there is a ruling social class in the United States. This class is made up of the owners and managers of large corporations, which means the members have many economic and political interests in common, and many conflicts with ordinary working people. Comprising at most 1 percent of the total population, members of this class own 25 to 30 percent of all privately held wealth in America, own 60 to 70 percent of the privately held corporate wealth, receive 20 to 25 percent of the yearly income, direct the large corporations and foundations, and dominate the federal government in Washington.

Most social scientists disagree with this view. Some dismiss it out of hand, others become quite vehement in disputing it. The overwhelming majority of them believe that the United States has a "pluralistic" power structure, in which a wide variety of "veto groups" (e.g., businessmen, farmers, unions, consumers) and "voluntary associations" (e.g., National Association of Manufacturers, Americans for Democratic Action, Common Cause) form shifting coalitions to influence decisions on different issues. These groups and associations are said to have differing amounts of interest and influence on various questions. Contrary to my view, pluralists assert that no one group, not even the owners and managers of large corporations, has the cohesiveness and ability to determine the outcome of a wide variety of social, economic, and political issues.

If my view is to prevail, four basic steps are necessary. First, it is necessary to present an adequate conception of what is meant by a "social class." Second, evidence must be presented to demonstrate that such a thing as a "social upper class" exists in the United States. Third, evidence and argument must show that this social upper class has leadership groups that can formulate policies on economic and political questions of importance to the class as a whole. Finally, it is essential to present evidence and argument concerning the several means by which leaders within the upper class are able to have their plans and programs adopted by the federal government. I will now turn to each of these questions.

What Is a Social Class?

There is in fact considerable agreement among social scientists as to what is meant by the concept "social class." E. Digby

Baltzell, a sociologist who has written two important books on the upper class, adopts the following definition from an earlier generation of social-class researchers:

A "Social Class" is the largest group of people whose members have intimate access to one another. A class is composed of families and social cliques. The interrelationships between these families and cliques, in such informal activities as dancing, visiting, receptions, teas, and larger informal affairs, constitute the function of the social class.[1]

Sociologist Harold M. Hodges employs the following definition in his widely used textbook:

[A social class] is a distinct reality which embraces the fact that people live, eat, play, mate, dress, work, and think at contrasting and dissimilar levels. These levels—social classes—are the blended product of shared and analogous occupational orientations, educational backgrounds, economic wherewithal, and life experiences. . . . Each of these likenesses will be reinforced in turn by clique, work, and friendship ties which are limited, in the main, to persons occupying the same class level.[2]

In a best-selling social-psychology textbook, similar phrases are used in defining social class: "A division of a society, made up of persons possessing certain common social characteristics which are taken to qualify them for intimate equal-status rela-

1. E. Digby Baltzell, *Philadelphia Gentlemen* (New York: Free Press, 1958), p. 78.
2. Harold M. Hodges, *Social Stratification: Class in America* (Cambridge, Mass.: Schenkman Publishing Company, 1964), p. 13.

tions with one another, and which restrict their interaction with members of other social classes."[3]

Marxists, the major opponents of the orthodoxy within American social science, would not disagree with these definitions. Paul Sweezy, in a discussion of the general characteristics of social classes, notes that they are "obstinate facts and not mere logical categories," and that "the fundamental unit of class membership is the family and not the individual." He concludes: "A social class, then, is made up of freely intermarrying families."[4]

The only dissenters from this conception of social class might be followers of Max Weber. Weber made a distinction between *class* and *status*, restricting *class* to mean a category of people with common economic opportunities and common life chances, and using the term *status* to refer to interacting social groups with common life styles. Thus, political scientist Robert A. Dahl, a pluralist, speaks of "social standing" instead of social class when he talks of interacting circles of people who treat each other as social equals, belong to the same clubs, mingle freely in intimate social events, and intermarry.[5] In short, what people like Weber and Dahl mean by "social standing" and

3. David Krech, Richard S. Crutchfield, and Egerton L. Ballachey, *The Individual in Society* (New York: McGraw-Hill, 1962), p. 338.

4. Paul M. Sweezy, "The American Ruling Class," *The Present as History* (New York: Monthly Review Press, 1953), pp. 123–124. However, Marxists would stress that social classes have their origins in the property system, in the relationship of various groups to the means of production. They also would stress the role of economic and political conflicts between these social groups in creating class ideologies and class boundaries. For a good discussion of the Marxian view, see T. B. Bottomore, *Classes in Modern Society* (New York: Pantheon, 1966).

5. Robert A. Dahl, *Who Governs?* (New Haven, Conn.: Yale University Press, 1961), p. 229.

"status group" are what most social scientists mean when they use the term "social class." In his textbook on social stratification, Joseph A. Kahl deals with this semantic problem very nicely when he concludes, "If a large group of families are approximately equal to each other and clearly differentiated from other families, we call them a *social class*." He then adds, in a significant footnote, "Here, obviously, we depart from the terminology of Weber in favor of ordinary English."[6] I too prefer ordinary English.

Is There a National Upper Class?

As noted, I believe there is a national upper class in the United States. Recalling the discussion in the previous section, this means that wealthy families from all over the country, and particularly from major cities like New York, San Francisco, Chicago, and Houston, are part of interlocking social circles which perceive each other as equals, belong to the same clubs, interact frequently, and freely intermarry.

Whether we call it a "social class" or a "status group," many pluralistic social scientists would deny that such a social group exists. They assert that there is no social "cohesiveness" among the various rich in different parts of the country. For them, social registers, blue books, and club membership lists are merely collections of names which imply nothing about group interaction.

There is a wealth of journalistic evidence which suggests the existence of a national upper class. It ranges from Cleveland Amory's *The Proper Bostonians* and *Who Killed Society?* to

6. Joseph A. Kahl, *The American Class Structure* (New York: Rinehart, 1959), p. 12.

Lucy Kavaler's *The Private World of High Society* and Stephen Birmingham's *The Right People*. But what is the systematic evidence which I can present for my thesis? There is first of all the evidence that has been developed from the study of attendance at private schools. It has been shown that a few dozen prep schools bring together children of the upper class from all over the country. From this evidence it can be argued that young members of the upper class develop lifetime friendship ties with like-status age-mates in every section of the country.[7]

There is second the systematic evidence which comes from studying high-status summer resorts. Two such studies show that these resorts bring together upper-class families from several different large cities.[8] Third, there is the evidence of business interconnections. Several different studies have demonstrated that interlocking directorships bring wealthy men from all over the country into face-to-face relationships at the board meetings of banks, insurance companies, and other corporations.[9]

And finally, there is the evidence developed from studying exclusive social clubs. Such studies have been made in the past, but the present investigation of the Bohemian Club, the Rancheros Visitadores, and the Roundup Riders of the Rockies is a more comprehensive effort. *In short, I believe the present*

7. Baltzell, *Philadelphia Gentlemen*, chapter 12. Domhoff, *The Higher Circles*, p. 78.

8. Baltzell, *Philadelphia Gentlemen*, pp. 248–51. Domhoff, *The Higher Circles*, pp. 79–82. For recent anecdotal evidence on this point, see Stephen Birmingham, *The Right People* (Boston: Little, Brown, 1968), Part 3.

9. *Interlocks in Corporate Management* (Washington: U.S. Government Printing Office, 1965) summarizes much of this information and presents new evidence as well. See also Peter Dooley, "The Interlocking Directorate" (*American Economic Review*, December, 1969).

book to be significant evidence for the existence of a cohesive American upper class.

The Bohemian Grove, as well as other watering holes and social clubs, are relevant to the problem of class cohesiveness in two ways. First, the very fact that rich men from all over the country gather in such close circumstances as the Bohemian Grove is evidence for the existence of a socially cohesive upper class. It demonstrates that many of these men do know each other, that they have face-to-face communications, and that they are a social network. In this sense, we are looking at the Bohemian Grove and other social retreats as a *result* of social processes that lead to class cohesion. But such institutions also can be viewed as facilitators of social ties. Once formed, these groups become another avenue by which the cohesiveness of the upper class is maintained.

In claiming that clubs and retreats like the Bohemians and the Rancheros are evidence for my thesis of a national upper class, I am assuming that cohesion develops within the settings they provide. Perhaps some readers will find that assumption questionable. So let us pause to ask: Are there reasons to believe that the Bohemian Grove and its imitators lead to greater cohesion within the upper class?

For one thing, we have the testimony of members themselves. There are several accounts by leading members of these groups, past and present, which attest to the intimacy that develops among members. John J. Mitchell, El Presidente of Los Rancheros Visitadores from 1930 to 1955, wrote as follows on the twenty-fifth anniversary of the group:

All the pledges and secret oaths in the universe cannot tie men, our kind of men, together like the mutual appreciation of a beautiful horse, the moon behind a cloud, a song around the campfire or a ride down the Santa Ynez Valley. These are experiences common on our ride, but unknown to most of our daily lives. Our organization, to all appearances, is the most informal imaginable. Yet there are men here who see one another once a year, yet feel a bond closer than between those they have known all their lives.[10]

F. Burr Betts, chairman of the board of Security Life of Denver, says the following about the Roundup Riders:

I think you find out about the Roundup Riders when you go to a Rider's funeral. Because there you'll find, no matter how many organizations the man belonged to, almost every pallbearer is a Roundup Rider. I always think of the Roundup Riders as the first affiliation. We have the closest knit fraternity in the world.[11]

Further testimony is perhaps superfluous, but here are the words of Roundup Rider president Rick Ricketson:

You may not see a man for a year, but when he arrives there on the ride it's like he left yesterday. And you have that feeling that he understands you and you understand him. There's not another association that I've had that brings men closer together.[12]

A second reason for stressing the importance of retreats and clubs like the Bohemian Grove is a body of research within social psychology which deals with group cohesion. "Group dynamics" suggests the following about cohesiveness. (1)

10. Neill C. Wilson, *Los Rancheros Visitadores,* p. 2.
11. Robert Pattridge, "Closer to Heaven on Horseback," p. 11.
12. Ibid.

Physical proximity is likely to lead to group solidarity. Thus, the mere fact that these men gather together in such intimate physical settings implies that cohesiveness develops. (The same point can be made, of course, about exclusive neighborhoods, private schools, and expensive summer resorts.) (2) *The more people interact, the more they will like each other.* This is hardly a profound discovery, but we can note that the Bohemian Grove and other watering holes maximize personal interactions. (3) *Groups seen as high in status are more cohesive.* The Bohemian Club fits the category of a high-status group. Further, its stringent membership requirements, long waiting lists, and high dues also serve to heighten its valuation in the eyes of its members. Members are likely to think of themselves as "special" people, which would heighten their attractiveness to each other, and increase the likelihood of interaction and cohesiveness. (4) *The best atmosphere for increasing group cohesiveness is one that is relaxed and cooperative.* Again the Bohemian Grove, the Rancheros, and the Roundup Riders are ideal examples of this kind of climate. From a group-dynamics point of view, then, we could argue that one of the reasons for upper-class cohesiveness is the fact that the class is organized into a wide variety of small groups which encourage face-to-face interaction and ensure status and security for members.[13]

13. Dorwin Cartwright and Alvin Zander, *Group Dynamics* (New York: Harper & Row, 1960), pp. 74–82; Albert J. Lott and Bernice E. Lott, "Group Cohesiveness as Interpersonal Attraction" (*Psychological Bulletin*, 64, 1965), pp. 259–309; Michael Argyle, *Social Interaction* (Chicago: Aldine Publishing Company, 1969), pp. 220–23. I am grateful to sociologist John Sonquist of the University of California, Santa Barbara, for making me aware of how important the small-groups literature might be for studies of the upper class. Findings on influence processes, communication patterns, and the development of informal leadership also might be applicable to problems in the area of upper-class research.

In summary, if we take these several common settings together—schools, resorts, corporation directorships, and social clubs—and assume on the basis of members' testimony and the evidence of small-group research that interaction in such settings leads to group cohesiveness, then I think we are justified in saying that wealthy families from all over the United States are linked together in a variety of ways into a national upper class.

Policy Consensus within the Upper Class

Even if the evidence and arguments for the existence of a socially cohesive national upper class are accepted, there is still the question of whether or not this class has the means by which its members can reach policy consensus on issues of importance to them.

A five-year study based upon information obtained from confidential informants, interviews, and questionnaires has shown that social clubs such as the Bohemian Club are an important consensus-forming aspect of the upper class and big-business environment. According to sociologist Reed Powell, "the clubs are a repository of the values held by the upper-level prestige groups in the community and are a means by which these values are transferred to the business environment." Moreover, the clubs are places where problems are discussed:

> On the other hand, the clubs are places in which the beliefs, problems, and values of the industrial organization are discussed and related to other elements in the larger community. Clubs, therefore, are not only effective vehicles of informal communication, but also valuable centers where views are presented, ideas are modified, and new ideas emerge. Those

in the interview sample were appreciative of this asset; in addition, they considered the club as a valuable place to combine social and business contacts.[14]

The revealing interview work of Floyd Hunter, an outstanding pioneer researcher on the American power structure, also provides evidence for the importance of social clubs as informal centers of policy making. Particularly striking for our purposes is a conversation he had with one of the several hundred top leaders that he identified in the 1950s. The person in question was a conservative industrialist who was ranked as a top-level leader by his peers:

> Hall [a pseudonym] spoke very favorably of the Bohemian Grove group that met in California every year. He said that although over the entrance to the Bohemian Club there was a quotation, "Weaving spiders come not here," there was a good deal of informal policy made in this association. He said that he got to know Herbert Hoover in this connection and that he started work with Hoover in the food administration of World War I.[15]

Despite the evidence presented by Powell and Hunter that clubs are a setting for the development of policy consensus, I do not believe that such settings are the only, or even the

14. Reed M. Powell, *Race, Religion, and the Promotion of the American Executive* (College of Administrative Science Monograph No. AA-3, Ohio State University, 1969), p. 50.

15. Floyd Hunter, *Top Leadership, U.S.A.* (Chapel Hill: University of North Carolina Press, 1959), p. 109. Hunter also reported (p. 199) that the most favored clubs of his top leaders were the Metropolitan, Links, Century, University (New York), Bohemian, and Pacific Union. He notes (p. 223 n.) that he found clubs to be less important in policy formation on the national level than they are in communities.

primary, locus for developing policy on class-related issues. For policy questions, other organizations are far more important, organizations like the Council on Foreign Relations, the Committee for Economic Development, the Business Council, and the National Municipal League. These organizations, along with many others, are the "consensus-seeking" and "policy-planning" organizations of the upper class. Directed by the same men who manage the major corporations, and financed by corporation and foundation monies, these groups sponsor meetings and discussions wherein wealthy men from all over the country gather to iron out differences and formulate policies on pressing problems.

No one discussion group is *the* leadership council within the upper class. While some of the groups tend to specialize in certain issue areas, they overlap and interact to a great extent. Consensus slowly emerges from the interplay of people and ideas within and among the groups.[16] This diversity of groups is made very clear in the following comments by Frazar B. Wilde, chairman emeritus of Connecticut General Life Insurance Company and a member of the Council on Foreign Relations and the Committee for Economic Development. Mr. Wilde was responding to a question about the Bilderbergers, a big-business meeting group which includes Western European leaders as well as American corporation and foundation directors:

> Business has had over the years many different seminars and discussion meetings. They run all the way from large public

16. For a detailed case study of how the process works, see David Eakins, "Business Planners and America's Postwar Expansion," in David Horowitz, editor, *Corporations and the Cold War* (New York: Monthly Review Press, 1969). For other examples and references, see Domhoff, *The Higher Circles,* chapters 5 and 6.

gatherings like NAM [National Association of Manufacturers] to special sessions such as those held frequently at Arden House. Bilderberg is in many respects one of the most important, if not the most important, but this is not to deny that other strictly off-the-record meetings and discussion groups such as those held by the Council on Foreign Relations are not in the front rank.[17]

Generally speaking, then, it is in these organizations that leaders within the upper class discuss the means by which to deal with problems of major concern. Here, in off-the-record settings, these leaders try to reach consensus on general issues that have been talked about more casually in corporate boardrooms and social clubs. These organizations, aided by funds from corporations and foundations, also serve several other functions:

1. They are a training ground for new leadership within the class. It is in these organizations, and through the publications of these organizations, that younger lawyers, bankers, and businessmen become acquainted with general issues in the areas of foreign, domestic, and municipal policy.

2. They are the place where leaders within the upper class hear the ideas and findings of their hired experts.

17. Carl Gilbert, personal communication, June 30, 1972. Mr. Gilbert has done extensive research on the Bilderberg group, and I am grateful to him for sharing his detailed information with me. For an excellent discussion of this group, whose role has been greatly distorted and exaggerated by ultra-conservatives, see Eugene Pasymowski and Carl Gilbert, "Bilderberg, Rockefeller, and the CIA" (*Temple Free Press*, No. 6, September 16, 1968). The article is most conveniently located in a slightly revised form in the *Congressional Record*, September 15, 1971, E9615, under the title "Bilderberg: The Cold War Internationale."

3. They are the setting wherein upper-class leaders "look over" young experts for possible service as corporation or governmental advisers.

4. They provide the framework for expert studies on important issues. Thus, the Council on Foreign Relations undertook a $1 million study of the "China question" in the first half of the 1960s. The Committee for Economic Development created a major study of money and credit about the same time. Most of the money for these studies was provided by the Ford, Rockefeller, and Carnegie foundations.[18]

5. Through such avenues as books, journals, policy statements, discussion groups, press releases, and speakers, the policy-planning organizations greatly influence the "climate of opinion" within which major issues are considered. For example, *Foreign Affairs*, the journal of the Council on Foreign Relations, is considered the most influential journal in its field, and the periodic policy statements of the Committee for Economic Development are carefully attended to by major newspapers and local opinion leaders.

It is my belief, then, that the policy-planning groups are

18. The recent work of arch-pluralist Nelson Polsby is bringing him dangerously close to this formulation. Through studies of the initiation of a number of new policies, Polsby and his students have tentatively concluded that "innovators are typically professors or interest group experts." Where Polsby goes wrong is in failing to note that the professors are working on Ford Foundation grants and/or Council on Foreign Relations fellowships. If he would put his work in a sociological framework, people would not gain the false impression that professors are independent experts sitting in their ivory towers thinking up innovations for the greater good of humanity. See Nelson Polsby, "Policy Initiation in the American Political System," in Irving Louis Horowitz, editor, *The Use and Abuse of Social Science* (New Brunswick, N.J.: TransAction Books, 1971), p. 303.

essential in developing policy positions which are satisfactory to the upper class as a whole. As such, I think they are a good part of the answer to any social scientist who denies that members of the upper class have institutions by which they deal with economic and political challenges.

However, the policy-planning groups could not function if there were not some common interests within the upper class in the first place. The most obvious, and most important, of these common interests have to do with the shared desire of the members to maintain the present monopolized and subsidized business system which so generously overrewards them and makes their jet setting, fox hunting, art collecting, and other extravagances possible. But it is not only shared economic and political concerns which make consensus possible. The Bohemian Grove and other upper-class social institutions also contribute to this process: *Group-dynamics research suggests that members of socially cohesive groups are more open to the opinions of other members, and more likely to change their views to those of fellow members.*[19] Social cohesion is a factor in policy consensus because it creates a desire on the part of group members to reconcile differences with other members of the group. It is not enough to say that members of the upper class are bankers, businessmen, and lawyers with a common interest in profit maximization and tax avoidance who meet together at the Council on Foreign Relations, the Committee for Economic Development, and other policy-planning organizations. We must add that they are Bohemians, Rancheros, and Roundup Riders.

19. Cartwright and Zander, *Group Dynamics*, p. 89; Lott and Lott, "Group Cohesiveness as Interpersonal Attraction," pp. 291–96.

Getting the Word to Government

We come, finally, to the question of how the policies developed in upper-class consensus-seeking organizations reach the government. There are a number of methods, all operating at the same time (and thereby increasing the potency of the message):

1. Many members of these organizations are appointed to government positions. "Over a third of the Council's 1,500 members," says a Council on Foreign Relations publication, "have been called on by the government during the last twenty years to undertake official responsibilities."[20] As for the smaller Committee for Economic Development, it always has three or four trustees who are listed as "on leave for government service." In 1961, for example, CED members were serving as director of the Federal Deposit Insurance Corporation, Assistant Secretary for Policy Planning in the State Department, and Administrator of the National Aeronautics and Space Administration. In 1970 the group supplied the government with the Chairman of the President's Blue Ribbon Defense Panel, the Special Representative for Trade Negotiations, the Secretary of the Treasury, and the Deputy Secretary of Defense.

2. Many members of these organizations serve on special commissions and committees appointed by the President to recommend policies on a specific issue. To take one small example from the evidence for this assertion, all eight of the most important postwar commissions concerning defense and economics were headed by men who were members of the Council on Foreign Relations.[21]

20. "Program and Purposes: Studies on Foreign Policy 1970–1971" (Council on Foreign Relations, 1971).
21. Domhoff, *The Higher Circles*, pp. 134–35.

3. Hired experts intimately identified with these organizations serve as government advisers. Thus, Henry Kissinger, closely affiliated with the Council on Foreign Relations throughout the 1950s and 1960s, served as President Nixon's chief foreign-policy adviser before becoming Secretary of State; Herb Stein, long-time economist for the Committee for Economic Development, serves as chief of his Council of Economic Advisers.

4. Members and employees of these organizations testify before government committees and serve as advisers to congressional committees.

5. Members of these organizations are fund raisers and big contributors to high-level politicians of both political parties, thus gaining what in polite circles is called "access" to the politicians in question.[22]

6. The books, journals, pamphlets, press releases, and speeches of these organizations are read with care by elected officials and/or their assistants because the social and economic connections of these organizations, along with their carefully cultivated "public interest" and "nonpartisan" images, have earned them a great deal of respect and status.

The Business Council

One of the policy-forming groups, because its big-business members have numerous off-the-record meetings with government officials, is worthy of further note in regard to the question of how upper-class leaders convey their opinions to government officials. This organization is the Business Council.

The Business Council was formed in June, 1933, at the sug-

22. Domhoff, *Fat Cats and Democrats*, pp. 151, 154–55.

gestion of prominent New York businessmen and bankers, as a quasi-governmental advisory group to aid the Department of Commerce. The little-known organization made a number of significant contributions to policy in the 1930s; its special committee on social security was especially important to the formation of the Social Security Act of 1936.[23] In the 1940s its members helped form the Committee for Economic Development to do the kind of research and discussion on policy matters which the Business Council was not equipped to undertake.

The organization really came into its own during the Eisenhower years. A number of its most visible members served in high-level posts in his administrations, and several articles about the council appeared in business periodicals. After disagreements with the Kennedy administration over modifications in its procedures which would have made the meetings with government officials more open to the public, the Business Council unilaterally withdrew from its semiofficial advisory status in 1962. It then reorganized as an independent business group available to consult with any department of the government. Its importance probably has increased, rather than diminished, since that time. The council enjoyed an especially close relationship with President Johnson.

In 1971 the Business Council had 197 members; 65 of them were in the "active" category and the rest were either "graduates" (those who had served their five years in the active category) or "honorary" (those graduates who were over seventy years of age). Active members, needless to say, do most of the work, although some graduates are called upon for advice and committee assignments. Membership on the Business Council is by invitation only, with new members being selected by

23. Domhoff, *The Higher Circles*, pp. 211–15.

the council chairman, the executive committee, and the membership committee. The members are, with few exceptions, the chairmen or presidents of the largest corporations in the United States. As of 1972, twenty-six of the fifty largest industrials were represented. So were major banks, utilities, and transportation companies.

The council has two forms of contact with the government. Best known are its four yearly meetings with government officials. Two of these meetings are two-day affairs in Washington, two are four-day gatherings in the huge Homestead Hotel, a quiet resort for the well-to-do in the tiny rural town of Hot Springs, Virginia, fifty miles from Washington, D.C. At these meetings council members hear speeches by leading government officials, conduct panels on problems of general concern, and talk privately with the government representatives in attendance. An added highlight of the Hot Springs meetings are golf and tennis tournaments as well as banquet-style dinners for members, guests, and wives. For the May 1972 meetings in Hot Springs the guest list included the Chairman of the Federal Reserve System, the Secretary of the Army, the Director of the CIA, the Secretary of Commerce, the Secretary of State, the Chairman of the Council of Economic Advisers, and a Special Assistant to the President.[24]

The council also connects with the government through its permanent liaison committees, which advise specific departments of the government. (Temporary committees are created from time to time to deal with special problems.) At present there are eight active committees. Typical are the Labor Com-

24. A detailed observational study of this May 1972 meeting was undertaken for me by Craig Kubey. See his "Notes on a Meeting of the Business Council" (*The Insurgent Sociologist*, Spring, 1973).

mittee, chaired by the head of the B. F. Goodrich Company; the Treasury Committee, chaired by the former chairman of Morgan Guaranty Trust Bank; the Housing and Urban Development Committee, led by the chairman of Kaiser Industries; and the Defense Department Committee, directed by the chairman of Monsanto Chemical Company.

Then too, council members often receive government appointments. There are, for example, 14 former Cabinet officers on the 1971 membership list. More generally, as of 1963 some 86 of 175 members had worked in the government on a full-time basis.

No one can state for sure just how influential the council is. Most government officials insist they merely "learn" from the meetings. Council members assert there is no "pressure" put on anyone; as they see it, the council is only a means by which they can make their information and their views known to government. "It's an easy mechanism to get our thoughts across," the chairman of Westinghouse Electric told one reporter. "Without it, you would have to somehow get an audience."[25] However, despite attempts to play down the role of the council, many of its members are willing to admit that personal contacts made through the meetings with government officials are highly useful. Some are able to give instances of where such individual ties were very important. R. V. Hansberger, until recently the chairman of Boise Cascade Corporation, claims that council members communicated the need for price and wage controls through links developed at the council.[26]

25. Frank V. Fowlkes, "Business Council Shuns Lobbying but Influences Federal Policy" (*National Journal*, Nov. 20, 1971), p. 2302.
26. Ibid.

On the other side of the business/government divide, there is the recognition that the council may have influence "by keeping top Administration officials advised on the expectations of the nation's largest corporations."[27] In the case of the wage-price controls referred to by Hansberger of Boise Cascade, Herb Stein of the Council of Economic Advisers noted, "Their views become a part of our information in policy making. It's a fact that the growing feeling in the Business Council of the need to do something on the inflation front was a definite contribution to the decision we took."[28]

For my purposes here, the exact degree of influence exerted by the Business Council is not a burning question. It must be seen as one of several avenues that leaders within the ruling class can take in communicating with government. However, there is one further piece of information, which suggests the Business Council is a major focal point at which the deliberations of the policy-forming apparatus of the ruling class are brought to government attention. This information concerns the degree of overlap which the Business Council has with other important groups. The council not only brings together the top leaders of the biggest corporations, but many of the same men who have discussed problems informally in settings like the Bohemian Grove, and more formally in organizations like the Council on Foreign Relations and Committee for Economic Development. To be specific, of the 197 active, graduate, and honorary members of the council in 1971, 31 were present as members or guests at the Bohemian Grove in 1970,

27. Ibid.
28. Ibid., p. 2307. For another recent discussion of the Business Council and its role, see Edward Cowan, "Secrecy in High Places" (*New York Times,* Oct. 29, 1972), p. 9.

49 were trustees of the Committee for Economic Development, and 42 were members of the Council on Foreign Relations. Taking the matter one step further, 9 of the 31 Business Council members present at the Grove in 1970 were trustees of the Committee for Economic Development and 7 of the 31 were members of the Council on Foreign Relations. (Two men, Harold Boeschenstein, the chairman of the board of Owens-Corning Fiberglas, and Philip Reed, a former chairman of General Electric, were present on all four lists.) In general, these interlocks suggest the possibility of a great deal of in-group communication while at the same time making it clear that the leadership group is not so small and tightly knit that every person can be a member of each organization.

One of the major criticisms that pluralists present of the ruling-class view is that the specific means by which leaders within the ruling class connect with government are never spelled out. I hope this section, particularly the information on the Business Council and its linkages, shows that such a criticism is readily answered.

A Final Analysis

The findings on the interlocks of the Business Council with the Bohemian Grove, the Council on Foreign Relations, and the Committee for Economic Development lead to a final consideration of cohesiveness within the American ruling class. Since the primary theoretical problem addressed by the empirical findings of this book is precisely that of ruling-class cohesiveness, it seems appropriate to conclude with a network analysis that demonstrates the interrelatedness of nine social and policy organizations dominated by the owners and managers of large banks and corporations.

For this analysis we utilized membership lists for six social clubs and three policy-planning groups. Two of the social clubs, the Bohemian Club and the Rancheros Visitadores, were the central focus of the first two chapters. The other four clubs are top-level clubs in Los Angeles, San Francisco, and New York: the California Club of Los Angeles, the Pacific Union Club of San Francisco, the Links Club of New York, and the Century Association of New York. In addition to these six clubs, the analysis included the three most visible policy-planning groups of the corporate rich—the Business Council, the Committee for Economic Development, and the Council on Foreign Relations.

Two factors limited the analysis to these nine organizations. One was the fact that few club membership lists are readily available. Indeed, the only other list I possessed at the time of the study was for the Detroit Club. The second limiting consideration was a desire to keep the number of necessary comparisons to a minimum in order to avoid the costly and time-consuming process of utilizing a computer for the data analysis.

The results of the study are found in the matrix on page 105. It presents the number of overlapping members among the six social clubs and the three policy-planning groups. This matrix shows, among other things, that the Bohemian Club has numerous interlocks with the other eight organizations; that the Pacific Union of San Francisco and the California Club of Los Angeles are closely related (96 common members); and that the Links of New York has many members in common with the Pacific Union (69) and the California (33). The matrix also reveals that the three policy groups have numerous members in common with all social clubs except for the Rancheros, whose members relate indirectly to the policy groups through their ties to

104

NUMBER OF OVERLAPPING MEMBERS FOR SIX SOCIAL CLUBS
AND THREE POLICY-PLANNING GROUPS

	*BO	PU	CA	RA	LI	CE	CFR	CED	BC
Bohemian (S.F.)									
Pacific Union (S.F.)	252								
California (L.A.)	136	96							
Rancheros (S.B.)	40	20	45						
Links (N.Y.)	67	69	33	1					
Century (N.Y.)	22	8	7	1	57				
CFR	34	25	15	1	108	332			
CED	20	24	17	2	60	23	52		
Business Council	27	24	14	2	77	12	42	49	

* Note: BO = Bohemian; PU = Pacific Union; CA = California; RA = Rancheros; LI = Links; CE = Century; CFR = Council on Foreign Relations; CED = Committee for Economic Development; BC = Business Council

the Bohemian Club, the Pacific Union, and the California Club. And, not surprisingly, it can be seen that the New York social clubs have the greatest number of connections to the New York–based Council on Foreign Relations. More generally, the analysis suggests that six social clubs and three policy-planning groups unite the dominant portions of the American business community into a social and communication network.

It should be emphasized that the interlocking overlappers presented in the matrix are not a big percentage of the total club memberships. The degree of overlap ranged from highs of 40 percent (Links Club and Business Council), 29 percent (Bohemian Club and Pacific Union), 25 percent (Business Council and Committee for Economic Development), and 23 percent (Century Association and Council on Foreign Relations) to less than one percent in the cases of the Century

Association with the Pacific Union, the Century Association with the California Club, and the Rancheros with the Links, the Century, the Council on Foreign Relations, and the Committee for Economic Development.[29]

But the interlocking members, however small their percentage of the total membership, are among the most prominent leaders in the ruling class. They are the people who span many interests and organizations, involving themselves in social, economic, and political decisions of major consequence in a variety of issue areas. For instance, the three men in the table with six interlocks apiece—Stephen D. Bechtel, John McCone, and Otto N. Miller—are among the most influential men in the western United States. Bechtel, the chairman of the family-held Bechtel Construction Corporation, is one of the five or ten richest men in the country. He is also a director of Morgan Guaranty Trust, Southern Pacific, Industrial Indemnity Corporation, California Shipbuilding Corporation, and Stanford Research Institute.[30] McCone, who was director of the CIA during the Kennedy administration, joins Bechtel as one of the nation's wealthiest men, and sits on such boards as United California Bank, Western Bancocorporation, Pacific Mutual Life, Standard Oil of California, and ITT. And Miller is the president of Standard Oil of California, the thirteenth largest industrial corporation in the United States as of 1969.

Thirteen men had five connections within the nine organizations studied. They include multimillionaires from New York,

29. These percentages of overlap were obtained in each case by dividing the number of common memberships in a pair by the total number of members in the smaller of the two organizations in the given pair.

30. See Burton H. Wolfe, "Bay Area Rapid Transit: Steve Bechtel's $2 Billion Toy" (San Francisco *Bay Guardian*, Feb. 14, 1973), p. 1, for a detailed journalistic account of the Bechtel family and its influence.

Ohio, Texas, and California, as well as the chiefs of such giant companies as Bank of America, Southern Pacific, General Electric, and Time Inc. Another 53 men had four interconnections. This group includes—in addition to multimillionaires and corporate heads—four top-level corporation lawyers from New York, Los Angeles, and San Francisco, and two university administrators. Generally speaking, the 1,070 men who constitute the entire matrix of interconnections were a cross-section of the country's major decision makers and their academic advisers between the years 1965 and 1970. The best-known among them are listed in the appendix, along with their interconnections, their occupations, and the major governmental positions they have held.

The network presented in this section is merely a glimpse into the cohesiveness of the American ruling class. The complete picture, which would include family connections, school cliques, attendance at summer and winter resorts, and corporate boards, as well as many more clubs and policy groups, defies easy analysis. It awaits a large-scale study utilizing computer capabilities. However, the enormous complexity of ruling-class networks can be grasped by a brief look at the hundreds of connections maintained by the members of just one organization we have studied—the Business Council.

For this particular analysis we tabulated all the links revealed by the 154 Business Council members who were listed in *Who's Who in America* for 1971–72. Our study of this information, which is not always complete information because it is self-reported, showed that these 154 men held 730 directorships in 435 banks and corporations. In addition, they had 49 foundation trusteeships in 36 different foundations, and 125 trusteeships with 84 universities. Further, they were members of dozens of major social clubs encompassing every region of the country. The 435 corporations represented at the Business Council were at the heart of the big-business community. One hundred seventy-six of them were among the 797 largest corporations, with many of those 176 coming from the top 25 for industrials, rails, banking, and insurance. The companies most heavily represented in terms of directors at the Business Council tête-à-têtes with government were the following:

COMPANY	BUSINESS COUNCIL MEMBERS
Chase Manhattan Bank	11 directors
Morgan Guaranty Trust	10 directors
General Electric	10 directors
General Motors	9 directors
Metropolitan Life	9 directors
First National City Bank (N.Y.)	8 directors
Corning Glass	8 directors
Goodyear	8 directors
AT & T	7 directors
Ford Motor	7 directors
General Foods	7 directors
B. F. Goodrich	6 directors
Pan American Airways	6 directors
U.S. Steel	6 directors
Mellon National Bank	5 directors
Sears, Roebuck	5 directors
Procter & Gamble	5 directors
International Nickel	5 directors
Boeing	4 directors
Chemical Bank	4 directors
Campbell Soup	4 directors

Continental Oil	4 directors
IBM	4 directors
First National Bank of St. Louis	4 directors
Eli Lilly	4 directors
Mutual of New York	4 directors
New York Life	4 directors
Southern Pacific	4 directors
Standard Oil of New Jersey	4 directors

In summarizing this section, I would contend that the information presented on the overlapping memberships among six social clubs and three policy-planning groups is good evidence for the cohesiveness of the American ruling class. I also would emphasize that the Bohemian Grove, with its many delights, and the Business Council, with its many governmental contacts, are two central points in a network of ruling-class institutions which embraces social interaction, business communication, and policy formation.

Conclusion

I began this chapter by expressing the fond hope that by the end of it there would be no doubt in anyone's mind as to the existence of a ruling social class in the United States, a ruling class made up of owners and managers of large banks and corporations. After defining what is meant by a social class, I argued that previous studies of prep-school attendance, summer resorts, and corporate interlocks, along with the new information presented herein on Bohemians, Rancheros, and Roundup Riders, are persuasive evidence for the existence of a socially cohesive national upper class. I then demonstrated that this social upper class has developed policy-planning organizations that concern themselves with developing solutions to problems of concern to the corporate rich. Finally, I tried to show the several means by which the plans and opinions of the leaders within these policy-planning groups are communicated to government. All in all, I think it makes a very good case for the hypothesis that the social upper class is a ruling class, especially in light of the amazingly disproportionate amount of wealth and income controlled by that small group of families.

But, alas, pluralists probably will not be satisfied. To their way of thinking, "power" can be demonstrated only by studying the individuals who initiate, modify, and veto specific policy proposals. They insist that we must trace a variety of issues from start to finish in order to establish our argument. They do not believe that power can be inferred from such indicators as wealth and income statistics, and from the kind of sociological evidence about the institutional framework of policy formation which I have presented in brief outline in this chapter.

The pluralists' single-minded way of studying power has a long and honorable history in American social science. Its roots are deeply imbedded in certain streams of philosophical thinking which try to tell us how science must be done. Empirical studies such as this book represents have little or no bearing on the arguments of this tradition. Until pluralists are able to abandon cherished assumptions which restrict the kinds of evidence they find permissible, or until power-structure researchers are able to complete a wide range of detailed case studies that show businessmen, lawyers, and employees from the Business Council, the Council on Foreign Relations, and the Committee for Economic Development in the naked act of making decisions, the argument about the distribution of power in modern America will remain stalemated.

In the meantime, however, let us agree that the rich live very well indeed even if we can't demonstrate to the pluralists' satisfaction that they are a "ruling class." After all, with their lavish Cremations of Care, their own private musical comedies, and their exclusive retreats, to mention only a few of their midsummer pleasures, they probably live just about as well as they could hope for if they were to be duly certified as an authentic ruling class:

"Great Owl of Bohemia, we thank
thee for thy adjuration.
Well should we know our living flame
Of Fellowship can sear
The grasping claws of Care,
Throttle his impious screams
And send his cowering carcass
From this Grove.
Begone, detested Care, begone!
. . . Once again Midsummer sets
us free!"

Appendix of Heavies

This appendix presents the most prominent men who were members of two or more of six social clubs and three policy-planning groups between the years 1965 and 1970. Less visible figures, including all those on whom no information was available in conventional sources, are excluded for reasons of space. Each man's affiliations among the nine organizations are noted. In addition, the person is identified where possible in terms of his primary occupation and the most important governmental posts he held prior to 1970.

Those who read through the entire appendix will be aware of several subgroups. The most obvious is a business one, anchored by corporation leaders, commercial bankers, investment bankers, and lawyers, and supplemented by public relations men, advertising men, stock brokers, management consultants, and accountants. Members of this large subgroup are found in all nine organizations. They are the heavies of the moneymaking world.

A second obvious subgroup consists of big-name experts. These men—primarily economists, political scientists, historians, and scientists—are the idea men and consultants for the rich and the powerful. Based at such elite universities as Harvard, Yale, and Stanford, they are the heavies of the academic world. They are found primarily in three of the nine groups—the Bohemian Club, the Century Association, and the Council on Foreign Relations. As noted, businessmen and bankers also are part of these three organizations, but with very few exceptions the experts are not asked to join such business bastions as the California Club, the Pacific Union Club, and the Committee for Economic Development. Most noticeable among the exceptions are university presidents—men that the big businessmen selected, in their capacities as university trustees, for these prestigious academic positions.

A third subgroup involves men of the media—correspondents, columnists, editors, and communications executives. Correspondents and columnists are confined by and large to the Century Association and the Council on Foreign Relations. Owners and managers of the media are in all organizations.

A final subgroup within this appendix comprises the cultural workmen—those who attend to the "quality" and "morale" of American society as museum directors, foundation executives, and consultants on the arts. Big businessmen connect with this group when they play their roles as "patrons of the arts."

Before plunging into this list, please keep the following cautions in mind:

1. I do not claim this appendix represents "the most powerful men" of the period 1965–1970. It is merely a good cross-section of the higher circles and their academic experts. Limited by and large to three major cities—New York, San Francisco, and Los Angeles—and three policy-planning groups, the network would have to include many other clubs and policy groups before it could pretend to completeness.

2. The men on this list have numerous other affiliations beyond those listed here. Indeed, to elaborate all the connections of these men would lead to a very detailed institutional mapping of the American power structure.

3. For reasons of space limitations, I did not include the full titles for all government positions. For example, men who served as "Assistant Secretary of State for Far Eastern Affairs" and "Assistant Secretary of State for Public Affairs" are identified alike as "Asst. Secy. of State." Readers wishing more details on the positions held by a particular person should consult *Who's Who in America, Who's Who in Finance and Industry,* and other biographical sources.[1]

4. The list is only guaranteed for 99 percent accuracy. Despite our considerable rechecking, there are bound to be a few mistakes. A handful of people may be missing from the appendix because we overlooked them or because we could not be sure that common names on two or more membership lists were in fact the same person. There also is the possibility that a few people appearing on the list are misidentified or given credit for an affiliation that belongs to another person of the same or a similar name. I apologize in advance for making such errors, but quickly point out that the very time-consuming task of eliminating all minor errors would not enhance the status of the basic findings that are established by the general results in large-scale investigations.

1. For a complete rundown on the biographical sources we use, see my section on "Personalities and Elites" in the *NACLA Research and Methodology Guide,* which is available for $1 plus 25¢ postage from NACLA East, Box 57, Cathedral Park Station, New York, New York 10025, or NACLA West, Box 226, Berkeley, California 94701. In the present study we made extensive efforts to locate information on each person but did not take the obvious next step with people we did not find—developing information via telephone interviews.

Lisa Young and Joel Schaffer did the basic work on this appendix. Peter Spofford and Kris Mailliard helped me check and recheck, especially in trying to track down difficult cases. Their help is gratefully acknowledged.

As in the matrix in the final chapter, abbreviations have been used for the six clubs and three policy groups. They are BO (Bohemian Club); PU (Pacific Union); CA (California); RA (Rancheros); LI (Links); CE (Century); CFR (Council on Foreign Relations); CED (Committee for Economic Development); and BC (Business Council).

APPENDIX OF HEAVIES

Name and Occupation	In-Group Connections			
	BO	PU	CA	RA
Brent M. Abel lawyer, McCutchen, Doyle, Brown & Enersen	x	x		
Herbert Agar journalist; author				
Hulbert S. Aldrich vice chairman, Chemical Bank New York Trust				
Malcolm P. Aldrich chairman, Commonwealth Fund				
Winthrop Aldrich former chairman, Chase Manhattan Bank				
Archibald S. Alexander lawyer				
Henry C. Alexander former chairman, Morgan Guaranty Trust				
Carl E. Allen vice president, General Motors				
William M. Allen president, Boeing Aircraft		x		
Frank Altschul former chairman, General American Investors				
Amyas Ames investment banker, Kidder, Peabody & Co.				
Lawrence C. Ames investment banker, Irving Lundborg & Co.	x	x		
Hoyt Ammidon chairman, U.S. Trust Co.				
Robert Amory, Jr. lawyer, Corcoran, Foley, Youngman & Rowe				

Major Government Positions

LI	CE	CFR	CED	BC	
	x	x			Special Asst. to Ambassador to Great Britain, 1943-46
x	x				
x	x				Special Asst. to Asst. Sec'y of Navy, 1942-45
x	x	x		x	Ambassador to Great Britain, 1953-57
x		x			Under Sec'y of Army, 1950-52
x		x			
x			x		Pres., Federal Reserve Bank of Chicago, 1956-61
				x	
	x	x	x		
	x	x			Officer, War Shipping Administration, 1941-44
x		x			
	x	x			Officer, C.I.A., 1952-62; Member, National Security Council Planning Board, 1962-65

Name and Occupation	BO	PU	CA	RA
O. Kelley Anderson chairman, New England Mutual Life				
Robert B. Anderson investment banker, Carl M. Loeb, Rhoades & Co.				
Robert O. Anderson chairman, Atlantic Richfield			x	
James W. Angell economist, Columbia University				
Ernest C. Arbuckle chairman, Wells Fargo Bank	x	x		
Hamilton Fish Armstrong editor, *Foreign Affairs*				
Herbert D. Armstrong treasurer, Chevron Oil	x	x		
Edward W. Arnold controller, Hydraulic Research & Manufacturing Co.	x	x		
Jack L. Ashby chairman, Kaiser Resources		x	x	
Victor K. Atkins president, Doran Co. (shipbuilding)	x	x		
William Attwood editor-in-chief, Cowles Communications				
J. Paul Austin president, Coca-Cola				
Lloyd L. Austin chairman, Security First National Bank			x	
George Backer president, George Backer Management Corp.				
Robert M. Bacon investment banker, E. F. Hutton & Co.	x	x		

Name and Occupation — In-Group Connection

118

LI	CE	CFR	CED	BC	
x			x		
x	x	x		x	Sec'y of Navy, 1953-54; Sec'y of Treasury, 1957-61
	x		x		
	x	x			
			x		
	x	x			Adviser to Sec'y of State, 1945
	x	x			Ambassador to Kenya, 1964-66
x			x	x	
			x		
	x	x			

APPENDIX OF HEAVIES

Name and Occupation

In-Group Connections

	BO	PU	CA	RA
Francis S. Baer former chairman, United California Bank	x	x	x	
Walter M. Baird accountant, Price, Waterhouse & Co.	x	x		
Walter C. Baker former vice president, Morgan Guaranty Trust				
Robert H. B. Baldwin investment banker, Morgan Stanley & Co.				
George W. Ball investment banker, Lehman Brothers				
Harding F. Bancroft executive, *New York Times*				
Paul Bancroft III investment banker, Draper, Gaither & Anderson	x	x		
Joseph Barber administrator, Council on Foreign Relations				
Harry M. Bardt executive vice president, Bank of America	x		x	
James M. Barker director, Sears, Roebuck				
Stanley N. Barnes judge, U.S. Circuit Court of Appeals	x		x	
Edward W. Barrett dean, Columbia University				
Dana T. Bartholomew former vice president, Alcan Aluminum				
Jacques Barzun historian, Columbia University				
Phillip Bastedo lawyer, Wickes, Riddle, Bloomer, Jacobi & McGuire				

120

LI	CE	CFR	CED	BC	
x					
x	x				
x		x			Under Sec'y of Navy, 1965-67
	x	x			Under Sec'y of State, 1961-66
	x	x			Division Chief, State Dept., 1945
	x	x			
	x	x			
					Asst. U.S. Attorney General, 1953-56
	x	x			Asst. Sec'y of State, 1950-52
	x	x			
	x	x			
	x	x			

APPENDIX OF HEAVIES

Name and Occupation	In-Group Connections			
	BO	PU	CA	RA
John B. Bates lawyer, Pillsbury, Madison & Sutro	x	x		
Leigh M. Battson director, Union Oil Co.		x	x	
James P. Baxter III former president, Williams College				
Gerald F. Beal chairman, J. Henry Schroder Banking Corp.				
Wellwood E. Beall executive vice president, Douglas Aircraft	x		x	
Kenneth K. Bechtel president, Marinship Corp. (insurance)	x	x	x	
Stephen D. Bechtel chairman, Bechtel Construction Corp.	x	x	x	
Stephen D. Bechtel, Jr. president, Bechtel Construction Corp.	x	x	x	
John R. Beckett president, TransAmerica Corp.	x	x	x	
Pierre Bédard cultural consultant, JFK Center for Performing Arts				
Frederick S. Beebe chairman, Washington *Post; Newsweek*				
Eugene N. Beesley chairman, Eli Lilly & Co.				
William S. Beinecke president, Sperry & Hutchinson				
S. Clark Beise former president, Bank of America		x	x	
David E. Bell vice president, Ford Foundation				

LI	CE	CFR	CED	BC
	x	x		
x		x		
x		x		x
x				x
x				
	x	x		
		x	x	
x				x
x		x	x	
		x	x	
	x	x		

Administrative Asst. to President Truman, 1951-52; Director, Bureau of the Budget, 1961-62; Director, Agency for International Development, 1962-66

APPENDIX OF HEAVIES

Name and Occupation	In-Group Connection			
	BO	PU	CA	RA
Elliott V. Bell chairman, McGraw-Hill Book Co.				
Karl R. Bendetsen president, U.S. Plywood-Champion Papers	x	x		
George F. Bennett investment manager, State Street Research & Management Co.				
John C. Bennett former president, Union Theological Seminary				
Louis A. Benoist president, Lawrence Properties Co.	x	x	x	
William Benton chairman, Encyclopedia Britannica				
Edgar Bergen entertainer	x			x
A. A. Berle, Jr. lawyer, Berle & Berle				
Simon Michael Bessie president, Atheneum Publishers				
Quentin W. Best president, Consolidated Rock Products			x	x
Benjamin F. Biaginni president, Southern Pacific	x	x	x	
John D. Biggers former chairman, Libbey-Owens-Ford Glass				
Reginald H. Biggs president, Raphael Weill & Co.	x	x		
Douglas M. Black chairman, Doubleday & Co.				

LI	CE	CFR	CED	BC
	x		x	

Asst. Sec'y of Army, 1950-52; Under Sec'y of
Army, 1952

| x | | | x | |

| | x | x | | |

| x | | | | |

| | | x | x | |

Asst. Sec'y of State, 1945-47; U.S. Senator from
Connecticut, 1949-53

| | x | x | | |

Asst. Sec'y of State, 1938-44; Ambassador to Brazil,
1945-46; Consultant to Sec'y of State, 1961

| | x | x | | |

| x | | | | x |

| x | | | x | x |

Minister to Great Britain for War Production, 1941

| x | x | | | |

APPENDIX OF HEAVIES

Name and Occupation	In-Group Connections			
	BO	PU	CA	RA
James B. Black former chairman, Pacific Gas & Electric	x	x		
William Blackie chairman, Caterpillar Tractor		x		
Edwin F. Blair lawyer, Hughes, Hubbard, Blair & Reed	x			
Roger M. Blough director, U.S. Steel				
Harold Boeschenstein chairman of the board, Owens-Corning Fiberglas Corp.		x		
Fred Bohen chairman, Meredith Publishing Co.				x
Charles G. Bolte vice president, Carnegie Endowment for International Peace				
Alfred R. Bone, Jr. vice president, American Airlines	x		x	x
John B. Bonny chairman, H. K. Ferguson Co. (construction)		x	x	
Dudley B. Bonsal judge, U.S. District Court, N.Y.				
Phillip W. Bonsal former ambassador				
Fred J. Borch chairman, General Electric				
Hugh Borton former president, Haverford College				
John Z. Bowers former dean, U. of Wisconsin Medical School				

LI	CE	CFR	CED	BC	
x				x	
		x			
x	x				
x		x	x	x	
x		x	x	x	
				x	
	x	x			
	x	x			
	x	x			Officer, State Dept., 1962-65
x		x	x	x	Member, Commission for International Trade and Investment, 1969
	x	x			
	x	x			

Name and Occupation	In-Group Connection			
	BO	PU	CA	RA
Robert R. Bowie director, Center for International Affairs, Harvard University				
S. F. Bowlby consultant, Bank of California		x	x	
Frank Bowles director of educational programs, Ford Foundation				
Hugh N. Boyd director, Associated Press				
Amory H. Bradford lawyer; vice president, *New York Times*				
Paul J. Braisted president, Edward Hazen Foundation				
William F. Bramstedt vice president, Standard Oil of California	x			
Roy L. Brandenburger vice president, Monsanto Chemical Co.		x	x	
Frederic H. Brandi investment banker, Dillon Read & Co.	x		x	
Alexander H. Brawner former president, W. P. Fuller & Co.	x	x		
W. P. Fuller Brawner former official, W. P. Fuller & Co.	x	x		
Henry C. Breck investment banker, J & W Seligman & Co.				
Kingman Brewster, Jr. president, Yale University				
Robert L. Bridges lawyer, Thelan, Marrin, Johnson & Bridges		x	x	

LI	CE	CFR	CED	BC	
	x	x			Planner, State Dept., 1953–55; Asst. Sec'y of State, 1955–57; Counselor, State Dept., 1966–68
	x	x			
	x	x			
	x	x			
	x	x			
		x			
x					
x	x	x			
	x	x			

APPENDIX OF HEAVIES

Name and Occupation	In-Group Connections			
	BO	PU	CA	RA
Ellis O. Briggs writer				
Detlev Bronk former president, Rockefeller University				
Melvin Brorby vice president, Needham, Harper, & Steers (advertising)				
Carl G. Brown, Jr. chairman, California Casualty Insurance	x		x	
Courtney C. Brown dean, Columbia University				
George R. Brown chairman, Texas Eastern Gas Transmission				
Robert M. Brown lawyer, McCutchen, Doyle, Brown & Enerson	x	x		
Zadoc W. Brown president, Brown Fund of Hawaii		x	x	
Paul M. Browne owner, Browne Travel Agency	x	x		x
George A. Brownell lawyer, Davis, Polk, Wardwell, Sunderland & Kiendl				
David K. E. Bruce former ambassador				
James Bruce adviser, Chemical Bank New York Trust				
Percival F. Brundage consultant, Price, Waterhouse & Co.				

LI	CE	CFR	CED	BC	
	x	x			Ambassador to Dominican Republic, 1944; to Uruguay, 1947; to Czechoslovakia, 1949; to Korea, 1952; to Peru, 1955; to Brazil, 1956; to Greece, 1959; to Spain, 1961
	x	x			
	x	x			
	x	x			Member, Commission for Trade and Investment, 1969
x				x	
x	x	x			Consultant, State Dept., 1946-57
x	x	x			Asst. Sec'y of Commerce, 1947-48; Under Sec'y of State, 1952-53; Chief, U.S. Delegation to Paris Peace Talks, 1969
x		x			Ambassador to Argentina, 1947-49
	x	x			Deputy Director, Bureau of the Budget, 1954-56

Name and Occupation	In-Group Connection			
	BO	PU	CA	RA
Gerald F. Brush president, Bruch, Slocumb & Co.	x	x		
Spencer Brush chairman, Brush, Slocum & Co.	x	x		
John M. Bryan president, Bryan Capital, Inc.	x	x		
Daniel P. Bryant president, Bekins Van Lines			x	
Hugh Bullock president, Bullock Fund, Ltd.				
McGeorge Bundy president, Ford Foundation				
Ellsworth Bunker former chairman, National Sugar Refining Co.				
William A. M. Burden partner, Wm. A. M. Burden Co. (investments)				
Carter L. Burgess former chairman, American Machine and Foundry Co.				
W. Randolph Burgess chairman, City Bank Farmers Trust				
Frederick Burkhardt president, American Council of Learned Societies				
Theodore S. Burnett chairman, Pacific Mutual Life Insurance			x	
Donald C. Burnham chairman, Westinghouse Electric				
Arthur F. Burns economist, Columbia University				
Hendry S. Burns former president, Shell Oil Co.		x		

Major Government Positions

LI	CE	CFR	CED	BC	
			X		
	X	X			
	X	X			Special Asst. to the Pres. for National Security, 1961-66
	X	X			Ambassador to Argentina, 1951; to Italy, 1952-53; to India, 1956-61; to Vietnam, 1967-
X	X	X			Asst. Sec'y of Commerce, 1943-47; Ambassador to Belgium, 1959-61
		X		X	former Ambassador to Argentina; Asst. Sec'y for Manpower, Dept. of Defense
	X	X			Under Sec'y of Treasury, 1955-57; U.S. Representative to NATO, 1957-61
	X	X			
X					
			X	X	
	X	X			Chairman, Federal Reserve Board, 1969-
X					

APPENDIX OF HEAVIES

Name and Occupation

Name and Occupation	BO	PU	CA	RA
James MacGregor Burns foreign service officer				
John L. Burns chairman, Cities Service Co.				
Louis W. Cabot chairman, Cabot Corporation				
Paul C. Cabot chairman, First National Bank of Boston				
John E. Cahill president, Cahill Construction Co.	x	x		
John R. Cahill vice president, Five-Fifty California Street, Inc.	x	x		
Richard E. Cahill officer, Cahill Construction Co.	x	x		
Asa V. Call former chairman, Pacific Mutual Life Insurance	x	x	x	
Cass Canfield chairman, Harper & Row, Inc.				
James Carmichael chairman, Scripto, Inc.				
Ralph M. Carson lawyer, Davis, Polk, Wardwell, Sunderland & Kiendl				
Henry Cartan partner, Porter Estate Co. (investments)	x	x		
Edward W. Carter president, Broadway-Hale Stores	x	x	x	
William L. Cary law professor, Columbia University				
Clifford P. Case former lawyer, Simpson, Thacher & Bartlett				

LI	CE	CFR	CED	BC	
	x	x			
x		x			
x		x		x	
x				x	
x					
	x	x			Special Adviser to the Ambassador to Great Britain, 1945
	x		x	x	
	x	x			
			x		
	x	x			lawyer, Securities and Exchange Commission, 1938-40; Special Asst. to U.S. Attorney General, 1940-42
	x	x			U.S. Senator from New Jersey, 1955-

Name and Occupation	In-Group Connectio

Name and Occupation	BO	PU	CA	RA
Everett Case president, Alfred P. Sloan Foundation				
John C. Case former vice president, Mobil Oil Co.				
John W. Castles III lawyer, Lord, Day & Lord				
Robert M. Catharine chairman, Dollar Savings Bank	x			
Jean Cattier investment banker, White, Weld & Co.				
Robert L. Chambers president, Bartlett-Snow-Pacific, Inc.	x		x	
Norman Chandler former chairman, Times-Mirror Co.	x		x	
Allan E. Charles lawyer, Lollick, McHose, Wheat, Adams & Charles	x	x		
Allen L. Chickering lawyer, Chickering & Gregory		x	x	x
Marquis W. Childs newspaper columnist				
Percy Chubb chairman, Chubb & Son (insurance)		x		
Walker L. Cisler chairman, Detroit Edison				
Howard L. Clark chairman, American Express Co.		x		
Thurmond Clarke judge U.S. District Court, California	x		x	
Lucius D. Clay investment banker, Lehman Brothers	x			

Major Government Positions

LI	CE	CFR	CED	BC	
	x	x	x		Consultant, State Dept., 1949; Chairman, Federal Reserve Bank of New York, 1962-68
	x	x			
x	x				
x					
x		x			
	x	x			
x		x			
		x	x	x	
x			x	x	
x		x		x	Military Governor, U.S. Zone of Germany, 1947-49

137

APPENDIX OF HEAVIES

Name and Occupation	In-Group Connection			
	BO	PU	CA	RA
Harlan Cleveland president, U. of Hawaii				
C. Wheeler Coberly vice president, California Cotton Oil Co.	x		x	
Dwight M. Cochran former president, Kern County Land Co.	x	x	x	
John P. Coghlan lawyer, Chickering & Gregory	x	x		
Charles W. Cole former president, Amherst College				
Peter Colefax chairman, American Potash & Chemical Co.	x		x	
J. D. Stetson Coleman director, Gulf Gas Corporation		x		
James S. Coles president, Bowdoin College				
Emilio G. Collado executive vice president, Standard Oil of New Jersey				
Charles Collingwood foreign correspondent, C.B.S.				
Harry Colmery investment banker, Glore Forgan, Wm. R. Staats		x	x	
S. Sloan Colt former chairman, Bankers Trust Co.				
James B. Conant former president, Harvard University				
Fairfax M. Cone former chairman, Foote, Cone & Belding (advertising)		x		
Joseph J. Coney president, Hillcone Steamship Co.	x			x

Major Government Positions

LI	CE	CFR	CED	BC	
	x	x			Ambassador to NATO, 1965–69; Asst. Sec'y of State, 1961–65
x					
	x	x			Ambassador to Chile, 1961–64
x					
	x	x			
		x	x		Special Asst. to Under Sec'y of State, 1941–44; U.S. Exec. Director, World Bank, 1946–47
	x	x			
x			x		
	x	x	x		Ambassador to West Germany, 1955–57
			x		

APPENDIX OF HEAVIES

Name and Occupation	In-Group Connection			
	BO	PU	CA	RA
John E. Connolly professor of surgery, U. of California School of Medicine at Irvine		x	x	
John T. Connor chairman, Allied Chemical Corp.				
Roger A. Converse airlines executive	x			x
Chauncey W. Cook chairman, General Foods				
Ransom M. Cook chairman, Wells Fargo Bank	x	x		
Donald E. Cooley business machines executive		x		x
Richard P. Cooley president, Wells Fargo Bank	x	x		
Reginald Coombe former vice president, Hanover Bank				
Philip H. Coombs director, International Institute for Educational Planning				
James F. Coonan chairman, Pacific National Life Assurance	x	x		
Robert B. Coons vice president, American Potash & Chemical Co.	x	x	x	
John Sherman Cooper lawyer				
Lammot du Pont Copeland chairman, Du Pont Corporation		x		
Andrew W. Cordier president, Columbia University				

LI	CE	CFR	CED	BC	
x		x	x	x	Sec'y of Commerce, 1965-67
x			x	x	
x	x				
	x	x			Executive Director, Materials Policy Commission, 1951-52; Asst. Sec'y of State, 1961-62
	x	x			Ambassador to India, 1955-56; U.S. Senator from Kentucky, 1946-48; 1952-55; 1957-
x		x			
	x	x			Adviser, State Dept., 1944-46; Executive Asst. to UN Sec'y General, 1946-61

APPENDIX OF HEAVIES

Name and Occupation

In-Group Connectic

	BO	PU	CA	RA
Ralph J. Cordiner former chairman, General Electric				
Stewart S. Cort president, Bethlehem Steel		x		
Aylett B. Cotton lawyer, Cotton, Seligman & Ray	x	x		
Tom B. Coughran vice president, Bank of America	x	x		
J. E. Countryman director, Wells Fargo Bank	x	x		
Hernando D. Courtwright president, Courtwright Corp. (hotels)	x			x
Norman Cousins editor, *The Saturday Review*				
Gardner Cowles chairman, Cowles Communications				
John Cowles chairman, Minneapolis *Star & Tribune*				
E. Morris Cox president, Dodge & Cox (investment managers)	x	x		
James F. Crafts chairman, Fund American Co. (insurance)		x		
Gordon B. Crary, Jr. investment banker, E. F. Hutton & Co.	x		x	
Sherman L. Crary treasurer, Bethlehem Steel	x	x		
Malcolm Cravens president, Cravens, Pargan & Co. (insurance)	x	x		
Charles W. Crawford president, Electric Equipment Co. of Los Angeles	x		x	

LI	CE	CFR	CED	BC
x				x
x			x	x

Member, Richard Nixon's Personal Campaign Staff, 1952, 1956

LI	CE	CFR	CED	BC
x		x		

Asst. Sec'y of Treasury, 1957-58

LI	CE	CFR	CED	BC
	x	x		
x	x	x	x	

Domestic Director, Office of War Information, 1942-43

LI	CE	CFR	CED	BC
	x	x		x
x				

Name and Occupation

In-Group Connectio|

Name and Occupation	BO	PU	CA	RA
Dana S. Creel former secretary; director, Rockefeller Brothers Fund				
Randolph Crossley president, American Pacific Life Insurance	x			x
Homer D. Crotty lawyer, Gibson, Dunn & Crutcher			x	
Philip K. Crowe conservationist; diplomat				
John H. Daniels chairman, Archer Daniels Midland Co.				
Norris Darrell lawyer, Sullivan & Cromwell				
Justin Dart president, Rexall Drug Co.	x		x	x
John Davenport asst. managing editor, *Fortune Magazine*				
Donald K. David former vice chairman, Ford Foundation				
Paul L. Davies chairman, FMC Corporation	x	x		
Paul L. Davies, Jr. lawyer, Pillsbury, Madison & Sutro	x	x		
Arthur H. Dean lawyer, Sullivan & Cromwell		x		
Eli Whitney Debevoise lawyer, Debevoise, Plimpton, Lyons & Gates				
Charles de Bretteville chairman, Bank of California		x	x	
William C. Decker former president, Corning Glass Works				

LI	CE	CFR	CED	BC	
	x	x			
		x			Special Asst. to U.S. Attorney General, 1953–55
	x	x			Special Asst. to Sec'y of State, 1957–59; Ambassador to South Africa, 1959–61
x			x	x	
	x	x			
x					
	x	x			
x		x	x	x	
x			x	x	
x	x	x			Special Ambassador to Korea, 1953–54; Chairman, Disarmament Conference, Geneva, Switzerland, 1962
	x	x			
x					
x		x			

145

Name and Occupation	In-Group Connectio

Name and Occupation	BO	PU	CA	RA
Christian Deguigne III president, Stauffer Chemical Co.	x	x		
Jean T. Delacour naturalist			x	
Frederick B. Dent president, Mayfair Mills				
Frank R. Denton director, Gulf Oil Corp.				
Emile Despres economist, Stanford University				
Richard R. Deupree former chairman, Proctor & Gamble				
Thomas E. Dewey lawyer, Dewey, Ballantine, Bushby, Palmer & Wood				
Byron Dexter editor, *Vermonter Magazine*				
Charles D. Dickey director, Morgan Guaranty Trust				
John S. Dickey former president, Dartmouth College				
William Diebold, Jr. economist, Council on Foreign Relations				
Phillip P. Di Giorgio director, Di Giorgio Corp.	x	x		
Robert Di Giorgio president, Di Giorgio Corp.	x	x	x	
Lowell S. Dillingham president, Dillingham Corp.		x		
C. Douglas Dillon president, U.S. & Foreign Securities Corp.				

Major Government Positions

LI	CE	CFR	CED	BC	
		x			
	x				
			x	x	
x				x	U.S. Treasury Dept., 1923-29
	x	x			Adviser, State Dept., 1944-45
x				x	Member, Commission on Foreign Aid, 1948
x		x			Governor of New York, 1942-54
	x	x			
x				x	
	x	x			Special Asst. to Sec'y of State, 1940; Director, Office of Public Affairs, State Dept., 1944-45
	x	x			
			x		
x	x	x	x	x	Under Sec'y of State, 1958-59; Sec'y of Treasury, 1960-65

Name and Occupation	In-Group Connection			
	BO	PU	CA	RA
George S. Dillon president, Air Reduction Co.		x		
J. Richardson Dilworth chairman, Rockefeller Center				
William H. Doheny director, Union Oil Co.		x	x	
Emmett E. Doherty Judge, Superior Court, Los Angeles			x	x
R. Stanley Dollar, Jr. president, The Robert Dollar Co.	x	x		
Charles Dollard former president, Carnegie Corporation				
James C. Donnell II president, Marathon Oil Co.	x			
Frederic G. Donner former chairman, General Motors				
Hedley Donovan editor, *Time*				
Jermone K. Doolan consultant, Bechtel Construction Corp.	x		x	
Goldthwaite Dorr lawyer				
Oscar J. Dorwin former vice president, Texaco, Inc.				
Howard W. Dougherty president, Trend Oil Co.	x		x	
Donald W. Douglas, Jr. president, Douglas Aircraft				x
Lewis W. Douglas former chairman, Mutual Life Insurance of New York				

LI	CE	CFR	CED	BC	
x					
x	x	x			
x					
	x	x			
x		x			
x				x	
	x	x			
	x	x			Special Asst. to Sec'y of Navy, 1942-45; Consultant to Sec'y of State, 1947
x		x			
		x	x		
x	x	x			Ambassador to Great Britain, 1947-50

APPENDIX OF HEAVIES

Name and Occupation	In-Group Connection
	BO	PU	CA	RA
---	---	---	---	---
Morris M. Doyle lawyer, McCutchen, Doyle, Brown & Enersen	x	x		
William H. Draper, Jr. investment banker, Draper, Gaither & Anderson		x		
John B. Ducato investment banker, Eastman Dillon, Union Securities & Co.	x	x		
Charles E. Ducommun president, Ducommun, Inc. (metals supply)	x		x	
Wallis B. Dunckel president, Bankers Trust Co.		x		
Herbert I. Dunn investment banker, Schwabacker & Co.	x	x		
Henry Duque lawyer, Adams, Duque & Hazeltine	x		x	
Vernon A. Eagle executive director, New World Foundation				
Fredrick M. Eaton lawyer, Shearman & Sterling				
William D. Eberle president, American Standard Inc.				
Rollin P. Eckis vice chairman, Atlantic Richfield		x	x	
William H. Edwards lawyer, Edwards & Angell				
John E. Elliott economist, University of Southern California	x		x	
Osborn Elliott editor, *Newsweek*				

LI	CE	CFR	CED	BC	
		x			
			x		
x					
x					
	x	x			
x		x			Chairman, American Delegation to Disarmament Conference, 1960
		x	x		
	x	x			
	x	x			

APPENDIX OF HEAVIES

Name and Occupation	In-Group Connecti			
	BO	PU	CA	R
William Y. Elliott political scientist, Harvard University				
Northcutt Ely lawyer	x		x	
Brooks Emeny former president, Foreign Policy Association				
Fred J. Emmerich former president, Allied Chemical Corp.				
Lester H. Empey senior vice president, Wells Fargo Bank	x	x		
Burnham Enerson lawyer, McCutchen, Doyle, Brown & Enerson	x	x		
Edward W. Engs, Jr. president, Engs Motor Truck Co.	x	x		
Morse Erskine II president, California Pacific Title Insurance	x	x		
Brantley M. Eubanks investment banker, Mitchum, Jones & Templeton	x	x		
Alvin Eurich president, Aspen Institute for Humanistic Studies	x			
William D. Evers lawyer, Allan, Miller, Groezinger, Keesling & Martin	x	x		
William Ewing, Jr. investment banker, Clark, Dodge & Co.				
Douglas Fairbanks, Jr. actor; producer				
Charles W. Fay investment banker, Glore Forgan, Wm. R. Staats	x	x	x	
Herbert Feis historian, Institute for Advanced Study				

152

LI	CE	CFR	CED	BC	
		x		x	Consultant, State Dept., 1958-63
					Asst. to Sec'y of Interior, 1929-33
	x	x			
x			x		
	x				
x		x			
	x	x			
	x	x			Economic Consultant, State Dept., 1931-37; Special Consultant to Sec'y of War, 1944-46

APPENDIX OF HEAVIES

Name and Occupation	In-Group Connect			
	BO	PU	CA	R
William O. Field, Jr. geographer				
Lawrence S. Finklestein dean, Brandeis University				
Thomas K. Finletter lawyer, Coudert Brothers				
Leonard K. Firestone president, Firestone Tire & Rubber	x	x	x	
John Fischer contributing editor, *Harper's Magazine*				
Gilbert W. Fitzhugh chairman, Metropolitan Life Insurance		x		
John Flanigan vice president, Anheuser-Busch	x	x	x	
Edward T. Foley president, Investment Operating Co.	x		x	
Ralph G. Follis chairman, Standard Oil of California	x	x		
Marion Folsom former treasurer; director, Eastman Kodak				
Henry Ford II chairman, Ford Motor Co.				
Claude E. Forkner professor of medicine, Cornell University				
Michael V. Forrestal lawyer, Shearman & Sterling				
Raymond B. Fosdick former president, Rockefeller Foundation				
William C. Foster former chairman, United Nuclear Corp.				

I	CE	CFR	CED	BC	
x	x				
x	x				Trusteeship Division, UN, 1946-47
x	x				Special Asst. to Sec'y of State, 1941-44; Sec'y of Air Force, 1950-53; Ambassador to NATO, 1961-65
x	x				
	x				
		x	x		Sec'y of H.E.W., 1955-58
			x		Member, Advisory Commission on Labor & Management Policy, 1961
x	x				
	x				White House National Security Staff, 1962-65
x	x				
	x		x		Under Sec'y of Commerce, 1946-48; Deputy Sec'y of Defense, 1951-53; Director, Arms Control & Disarmament Agency, 1961-69

155

APPENDIX OF HEAVIES

Name and Occupation	In-Group Connecti			
	BO	PU	CA	R
Henry H. Fowler investment banker, Goldman, Sachs & Co.				
Fred C. Foy former chairman, Koppers Co.	x			
Charles Frankel philosopher, Columbia University				
George S. Franklin, Jr. executive director, Council on Foreign Relations				
John M. Franklin former chairman, U.S. Lines Co.				
George C. Fraser former chairman, Texas Pacific Land Trust Co.				
John French lawyer, Curtis, Mallet-Prevost, Colt & Mosle				
W. Parmer Fuller III vice president, Pittsburgh Plate Glass	x	x		
Reed L. Funsten director, Standard Realty Co.	x	x		
G. Keith Funston chairman, Olin Mathieson Corp.				
Henry W. Gadsden president, Merck & Co.				
John Kenneth Galbraith economist, Harvard University				
John W. Gardner director, Common Cause	x			
Richard N. Gardner political scientist, Columbia University				
Milo S. Gates engineer, Swinerton & Walberg (builders)	x	x		

156

Major Government Positions

I	CE	CFR	CED	BC	Major Government Positions
x		x			Sec'y of Treasury, 1965-68
				x	
	x	x			Asst. Sec'y of State, 1965-67
	x	x			Adviser, State Dept., 1941-44
x				x	Officer, Transportation Division, War Dept., 1942-43
x	x				
	x	x			
x	x		x	x	Special Asst. to the Chairman, War Production Board, 1941-44
			x	x	
	x	x			Ambassador to India, 1961-63
		x	x		Sec'y of H.E.W., 1965-68
	x	x			Deputy Asst. Sec'y of State, 1961-65; Senior Adviser to U.S. Ambassador to the UN, 1965-67

157

APPENDIX OF HEAVIES

Name and Occupation	In-Group Connecti

	BO	PU	CA	R
Thomas S. Gates, Jr. chairman, Morgan Guaranty Trust				
Frank Gerbode professor of surgery, Stanford University	x	x		
Robert H. Gerdes chairman, Pacific Gas & Electric	x	x		
George F. Getty II director, Getty Oil Co.			x	
Harry D. Gideonse chancellor, New School for Social Research				
Carl J. Gilbert chairman, Gillette Co.				
Huntingon Gilchrist former director, Cyanamid Products, Ltd.				
S. Hazard Gillespie, Jr. lawyer, Davis, Polk, Wardwell, Sunderland & Kiendl				
Edmund S. Gillette, Jr. vice president, Johnson & Higgins (insurance)	x	x		
Roswell L. Gilpatric lawyer, Cravath, Swaine & Moore				
S. Everett Gleason historian, State Department				
Thomas F. Gleed president, Gleed & Co.	x	x		
T. Keith Glennan former president, Case Institute of Technology	x			
Robert F. Goheen president, Princeton University				
Harmon H. Goldstone architect				

LI	CE	CFR	CED	BC	Major Government Positions
x		x		x	Sec'y of Navy, 1957-59; Sec'y of Defense, 1960
			x		
	x	x			
x		x	x	x	Special Representative for Trade Negotiations, 1969-
	x	x			Foreign Aid Consultant, 1949-55
	x	x			
	x	x			Under Sec'y of Air Force, 1951-53; Deputy Sec'y of Defense, 1961-64
	x	x			Deputy Exec. Sec'y of the National Security Council, 1950-59
		x			Member, A.E.C., 1950-52; Administrator, NASA, 1958-61
	x	x			Adviser, State Dept.
	x	x			

159

APPENDIX OF HEAVIES

Name and Occupation	In-Group Connections			
	BO	PU	CA	RA
Arthur L. Goodhart former law professor				
Carter Goodrich economist, Columbia University				
Kermit Gordon president, The Brookings Institution				
J. Peter Grace president, W. R. Grace & Co.		x		
Reginald V. Grady president, Connell Brothers Co.	x	x		
Paul Grafe chairman, Grafe-Callahan Construction Co.			x	x
Richard A. Grant president, California Portland Cement Co.		x	x	
Spencer Grant, Jr. vice president, Marsh & McLennan (insurance)	x	x		
Joseph A. Grazier chairman, American Standard				
James C. Greene lawyer, O'Melveny & Myers			x	
Crawford Greenewalt chairman, Du Pont Corporation				
Donald M. Gregory, Jr. lawyer, Chickering & Gregory	x	x		
Joseph E. Griesedieck president, Falstaff Brewing	x			
Theodore A. Griffinger partner, Shuman, Agnew & Co. (stock brokers)	x	x		
Thomas Griffith senior staff editor, *Time*				

LI	CE	CFR	CED	BC
	x	x		
	x	x		
		x	x	
x		x		
x		x		
		x		
x				x
			x	
	x	x		

Consultant to the UN, 1948-51

Consultant to State Dept., 1946-53; Director, Bureau of the Budget, 1962-65

APPENDIX OF HEAVIES

Name and Occupation

In-Group Connections

	BO	PU	CA	RA
Peter Grimm president, Transmar Hotels	x			
John C. Griswold investment banker, Eastman Dillon, Union Securities & Co.	x	x		
Courtland S. Gross former chairman, Lockheed Aircraft			x	
Ernest A. Gross lawyer, Curtis, Mallet-Prevost, Colt & Mosle				
Alfred M. Gruenther director, Pan American World Airways				
Horace A. Guittard officer, Guittard Chocolate Co.	x	x		
Fred G. Gurley former chairman, Atchison, Topeka & Santa Fe Railway	x		x	
Robert J. Hadden director, American Mutual Fund, Inc.	x		x	
Harry L. Haehl lawyer, Lillick, McHose, Wheat, Adams & Charles	x	x		
Eric H. Hager lawyer, Shearman & Sterling				
Patrick E. Haggerty chairman, Texas Instruments				
Michael L. Haider former chairman, Standard Oil of New Jersey				
George W. Haight lawyer, Asiatic Petroleum Co.				
Najeeb E. Halaby president, Pan American World Airways	x		x	
Newton J. Hale chairman, Hale Brothers, Inc. (department stores)	x	x		

LI	CE	CFR	CED	BC	
	x	x			Special Asst. to Sec'y of Treasury, 1935–36
x					
				x	
	x	x			Deputy Asst. Sec'y of State, 1946–47; Legal Adviser to State Dept., 1947
		x		x	Supreme Allied Commander in Europe, 1953–56
				x	
x		x			Legal Adviser to State Dept., 1959–61
			x	x	
		x	x	x	
	x	x			
		x			Adviser to Sec'y of Defense, 1948–52; Deputy Asst. Sec'y of Defense, 1952–54

163

APPENDIX OF HEAVIES

Name and Occupation	In-Group Connections			
	BO	PU	CA	RA
Prentis C. Hale, Jr. chairman, Broadway-Hale Stores	x	x	x	
Stanton G. Hale president, Pacific Mutual Life Insurance		x	x	
Edward T. Hall headmaster, The Hill School				
Roderick C. Hall partner, McMicking & Co. (investments)	x	x		
Fowler Hamilton lawyer, Cleary, Gottleib, Steen & Hamilton				
Thomas J. Hamilton UN correspondent, *New York Times*				
Robert V. Hansberger chairman, Boise Cascade Co.				
Charles B. Harding investment banker, Smith Barney & Co.				
John D. Harper president, Aluminum Co. of America				
J. George Harrar president, Rockefeller Foundation				
E. Roland Harriman investment banker, Brown Brothers Harriman & Co.				
W. Averell Harriman former investment banker, Brown Brothers Harriman & Co.				
Eugene I. Harrington chairman, Honig-Cooper & Harrington		x		
Gregory A. Harrison lawyer, Brobeck, Phleger & Harrison	x	x		

LI	CE	CFR	CED	BC	
			x		
x	x				
	x	x			Special Asst. to U.S. Attorney General, 1938-42; Administrator, Agency for International Development, 1961-62
	x	x			
			x	x	
x	x				
x			x	x	
	x	x			
x	x				
		x		x	Ambassador to USSR, 1943-46; to England, 1946; Sec'y of Commerce, 1946-48; Under Sec'y of State, 1963-65
x					

APPENDIX OF HEAVIES

Name and Occupation

In-Group Connection:

	BO	PU	CA	RA
Joseph C. Harsch commentator, A.B.C.				
Dwight H. Hart, Jr. vice president, Allied Properties	x	x		
Fred L. Hartley president, Union Oil Co.	x	x	x	
William E. Hartmann architect, Skidmore, Owings & Merrill				
Broderick Haskell investment banker, Bache & Co.				
Caryl P. Haskins president, Carnegie Institution of Washington				
Gabriel Hauge president, Manufacturers Hanover Trust				
Alfred Hayes president, Federal Reserve Bank of New York				
Samuel P. Hayes president, Foreign Policy Association				
Robert M. Haynie president, Haas & Haynie (builders)	x	x	x	
Ellison Hazard president, Continental Can Co.				
John N. Hazard law professor, Columbia University				
Henry T. Heald former president, Ford Foundation				
Norman J. Hearn vice president, Union Carbide	x	x		
William R. Hearst, Jr. chairman, The Hearst Corp.	x	x		

LI	CE	CFR	CED	BC	
	x	x			
		x			
	x	x			
x		x			
	x	x			Consultant, Defense Dept., 1947-60; Consultant, Sec'y of State, 1950-
x	x	x	x		Special assistant to President, 1956-58
	x	x			
	x	x			
			x	x	
	x	x			Adviser, State Dept., 1941-45
	x	x			

APPENDIX OF HEAVIES

Name and Occupation	In-Group Connections

	BO	PU	CA	RA
August Heckscher former director, Twentieth Century Fund				
H. J. Heinz II chairman, H. J. Heinz Co.				
Harold H. Helm chairman, Chemical Bank New York Trust				
Wellington S. Henderson chairman, Henderson Boston Co.	x	x		
William G. Henshaw president, Henshaw Investment Co.		x	x	
J. V. Herd chairman, Continental Insurance Co.				
George Herrington lawyer, Orrick, Dahlquist, Rowley & Sutcliffe	x	x		
Christian A. Herter, Jr. vice president, Berkshire Life Insurance Co.				
Paul M. Herzog dean, Harvard University				
Theodore M. Hesburgh president, Notre Dame University				
James M. Hester president, New York University				
William A. Hewitt chairman, Deere & Co.	x	x		
William R. Hewlett president, Hewlett-Packard Co.	x	x		
James T. Hill, Jr. president, Inmont Corp.				

LI	CE	CFR	CED	BC	
	x	x			White House Consultant on the Arts, 1961-62
		x	x		
x		x			
x			x		
	x	x			Administrative Asst. to Vice President Richard Nixon, 1953-54; Policy Planning Staff, State Dept., 1954
	x	x			Chairman, N.L.R.B., 1945-53
	x	x			Chairman, U.S. Commission on Civil Rights, 1969-72
	x	x			
			x	x	
	x	x			Asst. to Under Sec'y of Navy, 1942-43; Asst. Sec'y Dept. Air Force, 1950-53

APPENDIX OF HEAVIES

Name and Occupation	In-Group Connection			
	BO	PU	CA	RA
Charles S. Hobbs vice president, Broadway-Hale Stores	x	x	x	
Harold K. Hochschild former chairman, American Metal Climax				
Philip Hofer curator, Harvard University Library				
Paul G. Hoffman former president, Studebaker Corp.; Ford Foundation			x	
Robert Hoguet executive vice president, First National City Bank of New York				
George Kenneth Holland president, Institute for International Education				
John B. Hollister lawyer, Taft, Stettinius & Hollister	x			
William L. Holloway lawyer, Morrison, Foerster, Holloway, Clinton & Clark	x	x		
L. Emmett Holt, Jr. pediatrics professor, New York University				
Herbert Hoover, Jr. consulting engineer	x		x	
Herbert Hoover III president, Digitek Corp.	x		x	
Paul E. Hoover chairman, Crocker-Citizens National Bank		x		
Garfield H. Horn lawyer, Sullivan & Cromwell				
Jack K. Horton president, Southern California Edison	x	x	x	

Major Government Positions

LI	CE	CFR	CED	BC	
	x	x			
	x	x			
	x	x	x	x	Administrator of Marshall Plan, 1948-50; Member, U.S. Delegation to the UN, 1956-57
x	x	x			
	x	x			Consultant on Latin America to Presidents Eisenhower, Kennedy, and Nixon
x					Member, House of Representatives, 1931-36; Director, International Cooperation Administration, 1955-57
	x	x			
	x	x			Under Sec'y of State, 1954-57
x					
	x	x			
				x	

APPENDIX OF HEAVIES

Name and Occupation	In-Group Connection			
	BO	PU	CA	RA
Harold B. Hoskins officer, Foreign Service Institute				
Preston Hotchkis chairman, Bixby Ranch Co.	x	x	x	x
Richard C. Hottelet correspondent, C.B.S.				
Amory Houghton former chairman, Corning Glass Works				
Amory Houghton, Jr. chairman, Corning Glass Works				
Arthur A. Houghton, Jr. president, Steuben Glass Co.				
Frederick L. Hovde president, Purdue University				
Jack H. How partner, Edward R. Bacon Co.		x	x	
Thomas C. Howe museum director, California Palace Legion of Honor	x			
John I. Howell chairman, Schroder Trust Co.				
George M. Humphrey former chairman, Hanna Mining Co.				
Gilbert W. Humphrey chairman, Hanna Mining Co.	x	x		
Reed O. Hunt director, Crown Zellerbach Corp.		x		
Phelps S. Hunter investment counselor		x		x
William N. Hutchinson, Jr. president, Wm. Hutchinson & Co. (stock brokers)	x	x		

172

Major Government Positions

LI	CE	CFR	CED	BC	
	x	x			
				x	
	x	x			
x		x		x	Ambassador to France, 1957-61
x				x	
	x	x			
		x	x		Member, Advisory Panel to Dept. of Army, 1952-60
	x				Member, White House Committee for Fine Arts
x		x			
x			x		Sec'y of Treasury, 1953-57
x			x	x	
			x		

APPENDIX OF HEAVIES

Name and Occupation	BO	PU	CA	RA
James N. Hyde lawyer, Hyde & deVries				
Robert S. Ingersoll chairman, Borg-Warner Corp.			x	
John Inglis investment banker, Blyth & Co.	x	x		
R. F. Ingold chairman, Los Angeles Investment Co.			x	x
Robert L. Ireland III investment banker, Brown Brothers Harriman & Co.			x	
John N. Irwin II lawyer, Patterson, Belknap & Webb				
O'Donnell Iselin trustee, New York Bank for Savings				
L. Otis Ivey director, Citizens National Bank of Los Angeles			x	x
Harry A. Jackson president, American Petrofina, Inc.	x	x		
George D. Jagels vice president, Investment Operating Co.	x		x	x
George F. James senior vice president, Mobil Oil Co.				
John K. Jamieson chairman, Standard Oil of New Jersey				
Philip C. Jessup judge, International Court of Justice				
Frederick O. Johnson president, Mountaineer Farms, Inc.	x		x	
Howard W. Johnson president, Massachusetts Institute of Technology				

LI	CE	CFR	CED	BC	
	x	x			
				x	
x					
x	x	x			Deputy Asst. Sec'y of Defense, 1957-58; Asst. Sec'y of Defense, 1958-61
	x	x			
x					
		x	x		
		x		x	
	x	x			Ambassador at Large, 1949-53
		x	x		Member, National Commission on Productivity, 1969-

Name and Occupation	In-Group Connection			
	BO	PU	CA	RA
Joseph E. Johnson president, Carnegie Endowment for International Peace				
Samuel S. Johnson president, Jefferson Plywood Co.	x	x		
Charles S. Jones former chairman, Atlantic Richfield	x		x	
Thomas V. Jones chairman, Northrop Corp. (aviation)			x	
Earle M. Jorgensen chairman, Earle M. Jorgensen Co. (steel manufacturers)		x	x	
John W. Jorgensen president, Earle M. Jorgensen Co.		x	x	
Devereux C. Josephs former chairman, New York Life Insurance				
Edgar F. Kaiser president, Kaiser Industries	x	x		
Peter H. Kaminer lawyer, Winthrop, Stimson, Putnam & Roberts				
R. Keith Kane lawyer, Cadwalader, Wickersham & Taft				
Frederick R. Kappel former chairman, AT & T				
G. E. Karlen president, Eatonville Lumber Co.	x	x		
Milton Katz law professor, Harvard University				
Carl Kaysen director, Institute for Advanced Study				

LI	CE	CFR	CED	BC	
	x	x			Officer, State Dept., 1942-47
		x			
	x			x	
				x	
	x	x			
	x	x			Special Asst. to U.S. Attorney General, 1940-42; Special Asst. to Sec'y of Navy, 1943-45
x			x	x	
	x	x			Solicitor, War Production Board, 1941-43; Special U.S. Representative in Europe, 1950-51
	x	x			Deputy Special Asst. to the President, 1961-63; Consultant to the Rand Corp., 1947-68

Name and Occupation	In-Group Connection			
	BO	PU	CA	RA
George E. Keck president, United Air Lines		x		
J. Ward Keener chairman, B. F. Goodrich Co.				
Dexter M. Keezer former vice president, McGraw-Hill Publishing Co.		·		
David M. Keiser president, North American Sugar Industries				
Paul B. Kelly director, Crocker-Citizens National Bank	x	x		
Louis O. Kelso author; lawyer, Kelso & Associates	x	x		
James S. Kemper chairman, Lumbermens Mutual Casualty Co.	x		x	
Marron Kendrick president, Schlage Lock Co.	x	x		
George F. Kennan author; diplomat; Institute for Advanced Study				
William J. Kenney lawyer, Sullivan, Shea & Kenney		x	x	
William Kent III president, Wm. Kent Estate Co.	x	x		
Clark Kerr chairman, Carnegie Commission on Higher Education	x		x	
John R. Kiely executive vice president, Bechtel Construction Corp.		x	x	
William D. Kilduff investment banker, E. F. Hutton & Co.	x	x		
James R. Killian, Jr. former chairman, Massachusetts Institute of Technology				

LI	CE	CFR	CED	BC	
				x	
x			x	x	
	x	x			
	x	x			
					Ambassador to Brazil, 1953-55
	x	x			Ambassador to USSR, 1952; to Yugoslavia, 1961-63
					Asst. Sec'y of Navy, 1946-47; Under Sec'y of Navy, 1947-49
	x	x			
	x	x			Adviser, Arms Control & Disarmament Agency, 1969-

179

APPENDIX OF HEAVIES

Name and Occupation	In-Group Connection			
	BO	PU	CA	RA
John R. Kimberly director, Kimberly-Clark Corp.				
Frank L. King chairman, United California Bank			x	x
Frederick R. King architect, Wyeth & King				
Grayson L. Kirk president, Columbia University	x			
Francis R. Kirkham lawyer, Pillsbury, Madison & Sutro	x		x	
Henry A. Kissinger political scientist, Harvard University				
Robert Kleiman editorial board, *New York Times*				
Gustav Knecht, Jr. investment banker, Dean Witter & Co.	x		x	
Douglas M. Knight vice president, R.C.A.				
Robert H. Knight lawyer, Shearman & Sterling				
Robert P. Koenig president, Cerro Corp. (mining)				
Joseph Kraft newspaper columnist				'
Henry R. Labouisse executive director, UNICEF				
Dan Lacy senior vice president, McGraw-Hill Publishing Co.				
Laurence Lane, Jr. publisher, *Sunset Magazine*	x			x

LI	CE	CFR	CED	BC	
x		x		x	
x					
	x	x			
x	x	x			
	x	x			Staff Member, National Security Council, 1961-62; Foreign Policy Adviser to President Nixon, 1969-
	x	x			
	x	x			
x		x			Deputy Asst. Sec'y of Defense, 1958-61
x		x			
	x	x			
	x	x			Member, State Dept., 1941-51; Ambassador to Greece, 1962-65
	x	x			

Name and Occupation	In-Group Connectio			
	BO	PU	CA	RA
Melvin B. Lane publisher, *Sunset Magazine*	x			x
William L. Langer historian, Harvard University				
Lewis A. Lapham vice chairman, Bankers Trust Co.	x	x		
Roger D. Lapham, Jr. insurance broker, Frank B. Hall & Co.	x	x		
Cramer W. LaPierre former vice president, General Electric	x			
Frederick G. Larkin, Jr. president, Security Pacific National Bank		x	x	
Sigurd S. Larmon former chairman, Young & Rubicam				
Roy E. Larsen vice chairman, Time, Inc.				
John W. Latham vice president, Fidelity & Deposit Co. of Maryland	x	x		
Hubert F. Laugharn lawyer, Craig, Weller & Laugharn			x	x
Reginald S. Laughlin lawyer, Wallace, Garrison, Norton & Ray	x	x		
John G. Laylin lawyer, Covington & Burling				
Fred Lazarus chairman, Federated Department Stores				
Ralph Lazarus president, Federated Department Stores				
Ivy Lee, Jr. president, Ivy Lee, Jr. & Associates (public relations)	x	x		

LI	CE	CFR	CED	BC	
	x	x			Research Chief, O.S.S., 1942–45; Asst. to Sec'y of State, 1946
x	x				
x					
x					
x		x	x		
x	x		x		
	x	x			Asst. General Counsel, Treasury Dept., 1933–35
			x	x	
			x	x	

APPENDIX OF HEAVIES

Name and Occupation	In-Group Connection			
	BO	PU	CA	RA
Barry T. Leithead chairman, Cluett, Peabody & Co.				
Theodore L. Lenzen vice president, Standard Oil of California	x	x		
Laurence E. LeSueur correspondent, C.B.S.				
John P. Levis chairman, Owens-Illinois Glass Co.				
Roger Lewis chairman, General Dynamics	x			
Wilmarth Lewis author		x		
David E. Lilienthal chairman, Development & Resources Corp.				
Alexander N. Lilley chairman, California Texas Oil Co.		x		
Franklin A. Lindsay president, Itek Corporation				
George N. Lindsay lawyer, Debevoise, Plimpton, Lyons & Gates				
John V. Lindsay former lawyer, Webster, Sheffield, Fleischman, Hitchcock & Chrystie				
James A. Linen III president, Time, Inc.		x		
Art Linkletter entertainer	x			x
Walter Lippmann newspaper columnist; author				

LI	CE	CFR	CED	BC	
x				x	
	x	x			
x				x	
x		x			Asst. Sec'y of Air Force, 1953-55
	x				
	x	x	x		Chairman, TVA, 1941-46; Chairman, A.E.C., 1946-50
		x			
	x	x	x		Staff Member, Defense Dept., 1949-53
	x	x			Adviser, State Dept., 1964
	x	x			Member, House of Representatives,1956-64; Mayor of New York City, 1965-73
x		x	x	x	
	x	x			

APPENDIX OF HEAVIES

Name and Occupation	In-Group Connections			
	BO	PU	CA	RA
Herbert S. Little lawyer, Little, LeSourd, Palmer, Scott & Slemmons	x			
Edmund Littlefield, Jr. president, Utah Construction & Mining Co.	x	x		
John E. Lockwood lawyer, Milbank, Tweed, Hadley & McCloy				
Ernest J. Loebbecke chairman, Title Insurance & Trust Co.		x	x	
Daniel E. London vice president, Western International Hotels	x	x		
Augustus C. Long former chairman, Texaco, Inc.				
Alfred L. Loomis president, Loomis Institute for Scientific Research				
George H. Love chairman, Chrysler Corp.				
Robert A. Lovett investment banker, Brown Brothers Harriman & Co.				
E. Herrick Low vice chairman, United California Bank		x		
Thomas L. Lowe president, Newhall Land & Farming Co.		x	x	
Alan J. Lowrey former executive, Union Oil Co.	x	x		
Charles F. Lowrey officer, Davis, Skaggs & Co. (stock brockers)	x	x		
Roy G. Lucks chairman, California Packing Corp.		x		
Daniel K. Ludwig president, Sea Tankers, Inc.	x		x	

LI	CE	CFR	CED	BC	
		x			
				x	
	x	x			General Counsel, Office of Inter-American Affairs, 1941–44
x				x	
x	x	x			
x				x	
x	x		x		Under Sec'y of State, 1947–49; Sec'y of Defense, 1951–53
x					
			x		

APPENDIX OF HEAVIES

Name and Occupation	In-Group Connection			
	BO	PU	CA	RA
Gage Lund chairman, Standard Oil of California	x	x		
Louis B. Lundborg chairman, Bank of America	x	x	x	
E. Wilson Lyon president, Pomona College			x	
Emmett W. MacCorkle, Jr. president, Air Reduction Pacific Co.	x		x	
Edmund B. MacDonald owner, MacDonald Products Co. (real estate investments)	x	x		
Robert D. MacKenzie lawyer, Graham, James & Rolph	x	x		
Donald Maclean president, California & Hawaiian Sugar Refining Co.	x	x		
Malcolm Macnaughton president, Castle & Cook (sugar, pineapples)	x	x		
George P. MacNichol, Jr. chairman, Libbey-Owens-Ford Glass	x			
Lincoln MacVeagh former ambassador				
Marshall P. Madison lawyer, Pillsbury, Madison & Sutro	x	x		
John R. Mage officer, Northwestern Mutual Life Insurance Co. of Milwaukee	x		x	
Robert A. Magowan chairman, Safeway Stores	x	x		
John P. Maguire president, John P. Maguire & Co.	x			

188

LI	CE	CFR	CED	BC
		x		
				x
x				x
	x	x		
x				

APPENDIX OF HEAVIES

Name and Occupation	BO	PU	CA	RA
John W. Mailliard president, Mailliard & Schmiedell (food brokers, importers)		x		x
Gordon Mallatrat vice chairman, Gulf American Corp. (land development)	x	x		
Walter H. Mallory director, Council on Foreign Relations				
Dean W. Malott former president, Cornell University	x			
Bayless Manning dean, Stanford Law School	x			
Edward M. Manning, Jr. president, Manning's, Inc. (restaurants, bakeries)	x	x		
Robert J. Manning editor, *The Atlantic Monthly*				
Frank L. Mansell investment banker, Blyth & Co.		x		
Stanley Marcus president, Neiman-Marcus				
Ernest S. Marsh chairman, Atchison, Topeka & Santa Fe Railway		x	x	
Burke Marshall vice president, general counsel, IBM				
Joseph A. Martino former chairman, National Lead Co.				
Birny Mason, Jr. chairman, Union Carbide				
Edward J. Mathews architect, Skidmore, Owings & Merrill				

In-Group Connections

Major Government Positions

LI	CE	CFR	CED	BC	
	x	x			Asst. to Ambassador to Petrograd, 1916-17
				x	
		x			Special Asst. to Under Sec'y of State, 1962
	x	x			
x					
		x	x		
x					
	x	x			Asst. U.S. Attorney General, 1961-65
x			x		
x				x	
	x	x			

APPENDIX OF HEAVIES

Name and Occupation	In-Group Connecti‹			
	BO	PU	CA	R‚
William C. Matthews senior vice president, Foote, Cone & Belding	x	x		
Marcus Mattson lawyer, Lawler, Felix & Hall		x	x	
Stacy May economist				
J. W. McAfee chairman, Union Electric Co.				
David H. McAlpin investment banker, Clark, Dodge & Co.				
Atholl McBean former chairman, Newhall Land & Farming Co.	x		x	
Thomas B. McCabe chairman, Scott Paper Co.				
Thomas McCance chairman, Manhattan Fire & Marine Ins.				
Dennis McCarthy lawyer, Van Cott, Bagley, Cornwall & McCarthy			x	:
John J. McCloy lawyer, Milbank, Tweed, Hadley & McCloy				
William James McClung general manager, Bethlehem Steel	x	x	x	
Leonard F. Mccollum chairman, Continental Oil Co.	x		x	
Marshall F. McComb associate justice, California Supreme Court	x		x	
John A. McCone chairman, Joshua Hendy International Co.	x	x	x	
Richard C. McCurdy president, Shell Oil Co.		x		

LI	CE	CFR	CED	BC	
	x	x			
x				x	
x	x				
		x	x	x	Chairman, Federal Reserve Board, 1948-51
x		x			
x	x	x			Asst. Sec'y of War, 1941-45; President, World Bank, 1947-4| Coordinator, U.S. Disarmament Activities, 1961-63
x			x	x	
x		x	x		Under Sec'y of Air Force, 1950-51; Chairman, A.E.C., 1958-60; Director, C.I.A., 1961-65
x					

Name and Occupation	In-Group Connection			
	BO	PU	CA	RA
Walsh McDermott public health professor, Cornell University				
Malcolm McDuffie vice president, Mohawk Petroleum Corp.	x		x	x
Neil H. McElroy chairman, Proctor & Gamble	x			
G. Thomas McElwrath western vice president, New York Life Insurance		x	x	
Garrett McEnerney lawyer, McEnerney & Jacobs	x	x		
Ross A. McFarland environmental safety professor, Harvard University				
George C. McGhee owner, McGhee Oil Production Co.				
James H. McGraw, Jr. chairman, McGraw-Hill Publishing Co.				
Raymond A. McGuire vice president, Pacific Employers Insurance Co.	x		x	
Thomas G. McGuire president, Industrial Indemnity Corp.	x	x	x	
Porter McKeever president, United Nations Association of the United States				
Robert M. McKinney publisher, Santa Fe *New Mexican*				
Norman L. McLaren accountant, Haskins & Sells	x	x		
Donald H. McLaughlin former chairman, Homestake Mining Co.	x	x		
Joseph R. McMicking partner, McMicking & Co. (investments)	x	x		

LI	CE	CFR	CED	BC	
	x	x			
x			x	x	Sec'y of Defense, 1957–59
	x	x			Consultant, Dept. of Army, 1951
	x	x	x	x	Ambassador to Turkey, 1951–53; to West Germany, 1963–68; Ambassador-at-Large, 1968–
x	x	x	x		
	x	x	x		Information Officer, U.S. Mission to the UN, 1947–52
x	x	x			Ambassador to Switzerland, 1961–63
x					Treasurer, UN Conference, 1945
	x	x			

Name and Occupation	In-Group Connection			
	BO	PU	CA	RA
John P. McWilliams former chairman, Youngstown Steel Door Co.				
Edgar N. Meakin president, California Pellet Mill Co.	x	x		
Fred H. Merrill former president, Fireman's Fund Insurance Co.	x	x		
John L. Merrill president, Merrill Estate Co. (investments)	x	x		x
John B. Merritt president, Byron Jackson, Inc. (oil equipment)			x	x
Schuyler Merritt II chairman, American Reciprocal Insurance		x		
Charles Merz former editor, *New York Times*				
John M. Meyer, Jr. chairman, Morgan Guaranty Trust				
Theodore K. Meyer lawyer, Brobeck, Phleger & Harrison	x	x		
Wilson Meyer chairman, Wilson & George Meyer Co.	x	x	x	
Sig Mickelson former executive, Time, Inc.				
Jeremiah Milbank director, Southern Railway	x			
Richard W. Millar investment banker, Glore Forgan, Wm. R. Staats	x		x	
Francis P. Miller director, Freedom House				
G. Willard Miller investment banker, Dean Witter & Co.	x	x		

LI	CE	CFR	CED	BC
x				x
	x			
x				
	x	x		
x		x		
	x	x		
x				
	x	x		

Consultant, State Dept., 1951-52; Special Asst., State Dept., 1961-65

APPENDIX OF HEAVIES

Name and Occupation	In-Group Connection			
	BO	PU	CA	RA
J. Irwin Miller chairman, Cummins Engine Co.				
Otto N. Miller president, Standard Oil of California	x	x	x	
Paul A. Miller executive vice president, Pacific Lighting Co.	x	x		
Robert W. Miller chairman, Pacific Lighting Co.	x	x	x	
William J. Miller book editor, Time, Inc.				
Bradford Mills investment banker, New York Securities Co.				
George G. Montgomery former chairman, Kern County Land Co.	x	x		
George S. Moore chairman, First National City Bank of New York				
Hugh Moore chairman, Dixie Cup Co.				
James R. Moore lawyer, Cooper, White & Cooper	x	x		
Joseph A. Moore, Jr. president, Moore Dry Dock Co.	x	x		
Maurice T. Moore lawyer, Cravath, Swaine & Moore				
William T. Moore chairman, Moore-McCormack Lines		x		
William H. Mordy chairman, Ambord Corp. (holding company)	x	x	x	
Carlton G. Morehouse vice president, Marsh & McLennan (insurance)	x		x	

LI	CE	CFR	CED	BC	
x		x	x	x	
x			x	x	
x					
	x	x			
x		x			
x				x	
x		x			
	x	x			Member, U.S. Commission on NATO, 1961
	x	x			
		x			

APPENDIX OF HEAVIES

Name and Occupation	In-Group Connection			
	BO	PU	CA	RA
Henry S. Morgan investment banker, Morgan Stanley & Co.	x	x		
Howard J. Morgens president, Proctor & Gamble	x			
Grinell Morris former president, Empire Trust Co.				
Lloyd N. Morrissett vice president, Carnegie Corporation				
David A. Morse director, International Labor Office				
Charles G. Mortimer chairman, General Foods				
C. C. Moseley chairman, Grand Central Aircraft Co.			x	x
Philip E. Mosely international relations professor, Columbia University				
Bill D. Moyers publisher, *Newsday*				
Henry T. Mudd chairman, Cyprus Mines Co.	x		x	
Malcolm Muir former chairman, Washington Post-Newsweek Co.				
Raymon H. Mulford president, Owens-Illinois Glass Co.				
William C. Mullendore former chairman, Southern California Edison	x		x	
Vernon Munroe, Jr. lawyer, White & Case				
Franklin D. Murphy chairman, Times Mirror Co.			x	

LI	CE	CFR	CED	BC	
x	x	x			
x				x	
	x	x			
	x	x			
	x	x			Asst. Sec'y of Labor, 1945–47
x				x	
	x	x			Officer, State Dept., 1942–46
		x	x		Assoc. Director, Peace Corps, 1961–63; Special Asst. to President Johnson, 1963–67
		x			
x		x	x		
x			x		
	x	x			
	x	x	x		Member, Foreign Intelligence Advisory Board, 1969–

APPENDIX OF HEAVIES

Name and Occupation	In-Group Connection			
	BO	PU	CA	RA
Grayson Murphy lawyer, Shearman & Sterling				
James L. Murphy investment banker, Reynolds & Co.	x	x		
Stanwood A. Murphy president, Pacific Lumber Co.	x	x		
W. J. Murray former president, McKesson & Robbins				
James Mussatti consultant, California Chamber of Commerce	x		x	
John W. Nason president, Carleton College				
Robert R. Nathan president, Robert R. Nathan Associates (consulting economists)				
John Nauman president, Kingwell Bros. Ltd. (bearings)	x	x		
Alfred C. Neal president, Committee for Economic Development				
Alexander C. Neave lawyer, Fish, Richardson & Neave				
Clifford C. Nelson president, The American Assembly				
Fred M. Nelson former chairman, Texas Gulf Sulphur				
Quigg Newton president, Commonwealth Fund				
Thomas S. Nichols former chairman, Olin Mathieson Corp.				
William I. Nichols publisher, *This Week Magazine*				

202

Major Government Positions

LI	CE	CFR	CED	BC	
x		x			
x			x	x	
	x	x			
		x	x		
		x	x		Adviser, O.E.O., 1965-68; Member, Commission on International Trade and Investment, 1969
x	x				
	x	x			
x		x			
	x	x			
x		x			Member, American Mission to Great Britain, 1941-45
	x	x			

Name and Occupation	In-Group Connection			
	BO	PU	CA	RA
A. L. Nickerson chairman, Mobil Oil Co.				
Waldemar A. Nielsen president, African-American Institute				
Louis W. Niggeman president, Fireman's Fund Insurance Co.	x	x		
Paul Nitze former investment banker				
Robert F. Niven secretary, Union Oil Co.	x		x	
Richard M. Nixon former lawyer, Nixon, Mudge, Rose, Guthrie, Alexander & Mitchell	x			
Lauris Norstad chairman, Owens-Corning Fiberglas Corp.				
Frank W. Notestein former president, Population Council				
Charles F. Noyes former consultant, Rockefeller Brothers Fund				
Frank G. Noyes president, Frank G. Noyes Co.	x	x		
Nicholas H. Noyes director, Eli Lilly & Co.				
John B. Oakes editor, *New York Times*				
James F. Oates, Jr. chairman, Equitable Life Assurance Society				
George J. O'Brien vice president, American Cement Corp.	x	x	x	x

LI	CE	CFR	CED	BC	
		x		x	
	x	x			Special Asst. to Sec'y of Commerce, 1947–48; Consultant, State Dept., 1966–68
x	x	x			Director, Policy Planning, State Dept., 1950–53; Asst. Sec'y of Defense, 1961–63; Sec'y of Navy, 1963–67; Deputy Sec'y of Defense, 1967–69
x					Vice President of the United States, 1952–60; President of the United States, 1968–
x		x			Supreme Allied Commander in Europe, 1956–63
	x	x			
	x	x			Asst. to Sec'y of State, 1945–46; Member, National Security Council Staff, 1951–53
x				x	
	x	x			
x	x		x		

Name and Occupation	In-Group Connection			
	BO	PU	CA	RA
Charles Odegaard president, University of Washington	x			
Reno Odlin chairman, Puget Sound National Bank	x	x		
Robert S. Oelman chairman, National Cash Register Co.				
Alfred Ogden lawyer, Alexander & Green				
John O'Melveny lawyer, O'Melveny & Myers	x	x	x	x
Andrew D. Orrick lawyer, Orrick, Dahlquist, Rowley & Sutcliffe	x	x		
William H. Orrick, Jr. lawyer, Orrick, Dahlquist, Rowley & Sutcliffe	x	x		
Frederick Osborn former president, Population Council				
William H. Osborn investment banker, Lehman Brothers				
Stanley deJ. Osborne investment banker, Lazard Freres & Co.				
Alfred P. Otto owner, Cavalier & Otto (stock brokers)	x	x		
Andrew N. Overby investment banker, First Boston Corporation				
Douglas W. Overton president, Japan-American Institute				
Eugene Overton lawyer, Overton, Lyman & Prince	x		x	
Frank Pace, Jr. former chairman, General Dynamics	x			

Major Government Positions

CE	CFR	CED	BC	
x				
	x	x	x	
x	x			
				Member, S.E.C., 1955-60
				Asst. U.S. Attorney General, 1961-65
x	x			
x	x			
	x	x		Member, Advisory Commission on Supersonic Transport, 1964
x	x			
x	x			Officer, State Dept., 1950-52
	x			Sec'y of Army, 1950-53; Member, Foreign Intelligence Advisory Board, 1969-

Name and Occupation	In-Group Connecti

	BO	PU	CA	R
David Packard chairman, Hewlett-Packard	x	x		
John R. Page president, General Steamship Corp.	x	x		
Robert G. Page chairman, Phelps Dodge Corp.				
George L. Parkhurst vice president, Standard Oil of California	x	x		
John C. Parsons lawyer, Robinson, Robinson & Cole				
Nathaniel Paschall chairman, Fidelity Northwest Insurance		x	x	
Ellmore C. Patterson president, Morgan Guaranty Trust				
Herbert P. Patterson president, Chase Manhattan Bank				
William A. Patterson former chairman, United Air Lines	x	x		
Thomas F. Patton chairman, Republic Steel				
Lee G. Paul lawyer, Paul, Hastings, Janofsky & Walker			x	
Edwin W. Pauley chairman, Pauley Petroleum	x			
Frederick B. Payne investment banker, Anthony & R. L. Day				
Charles S. Payson chairman, Vitro Corp. (engineering, ore refining)				
Thomas P. Peardon political scientist, Columbia University				

Major Government Positions

LI	CE	CFR	CED	BC	
x			x	x	Deputy Sec'y of Defense, 1969-72
	x	x			
		x			
	x	x			Lawyer, War Production Board, 1943-45
x		x			
x		x			
			x		
x				x	
			x		Member, U.S. Reparations Commission, 1945-47
x	x	x			
x		x			
	x	x			

APPENDIX OF HEAVIES

Name and Occupation	In-Group Connect			
	BO	PU	CA	R
Paul G. Pennoyer lawyer, White & Case	x			
Robert M. Pennoyer lawyer, Patterson, Belknap & Webb				
W. G. Peoples senior vice president, Southern Pacific	x		x	
Courtland D. Perkins aeronautical engineer, Princeton University				
James A. Perkins president, Cornell University				
Howard C. Petersen chairman, Fidelity Bank of Philadelphia				
Rudolph A. Peterson president, Bank of America	x	x	x	
George H. Pfau, Jr. investment banker, White, Weld & Co.	x	x		
Paul A. Pflueger partner, Pflueger & Baerwald (stock brokers)	x	x	x	
Herman Phleger lawyer, Brobeck, Phleger & Harrison	x	x	x	
Gerard Piel publisher, *Scientific American*				
Roland Pierotti executive vice president, Bank of America		x		
Warren L. Pierson former chairman, American Cables & Radio	x			
Alan Pifer president, Carnegie Corporation				
H. Harvey Pike partner, H. H. Pike & Co. (commodity brokers)				

Major Government Positions

LI	CE	CFR	CED	BC	
x	x	x			
x	x	x			Staff Member, Defense Dept., 1955–58
	x	x			Chief Scientist, U.S. Air Force, 1956–57
	x	x			Chairman, Commission on Foreign Assistance Programs, 1965
		x	x		Asst. Sec'y of War, 1945–47; Special Asst. to the President on Trade Relations, 1961–62
x			x		
x		x			Legal Adviser, State Dept., 1953–57
	x	x			
		x			Lawyer, S.E.C., 1937–47
x		x			
	x	x			Consultant to the President on Educational Finance, 1969
	x	x			

211

Name and Occupation	In-Group Connect		
	BO	PU	CA
John J. Pike chairman, Lift Systems, Inc.	x		x
Thomas P. Pike chairman, Pike Oil Drilling Co.	x		x
Christian W. Planje president, R. E. Case & Co. (management consultants)		x	x
Calvin H. Plimpton president, Amherst College			
Francis Plimpton lawyer, Debevoise, Plimpton, Lyons & Gates			
L. Welch Pogue lawyer, Reavis, Pogue, Neal & Rose	x		
A. E. Ponting investment banker, Blyth & Co.	x	x	
George A. Poole president, Intercompany Corp.	x	x	
John E. Porter treasurer, McCreary-Koretsky Engineering		x	
Robert S. Potter lawyer, Patterson, Belknap & Webb			
Stanley Powell, Jr. president, Matson Navigation Co.	x	x	
Don K. Price, Jr. dean, Harvard University			
Gwilym A. Price former chairman, Westinghouse Electric			
Frank O. Prior former chairman, Standard Oil of Indiana	x	x	
Nathan M. Pusey president, Harvard University			

Major Government Positions

LI	CE	CFR	CED	BC	
					Asst. Sec'y of Defense, 1953-54; Special Asst. to the President, 1954-58
	x	x			
	x	x			Deputy U.S. Representative to UN, 1961-65
		x			
	x				
	x	x			
	x	x			Consultant, White House, 1961
x				x	
x					
	x	x			

APPENDIX OF HEAVIES

Name and Occupation	In-Group Connecti

Name and Occupation	BO	PU	CA	R.
Charles H. Quinn chairman, Electric Products Corp.	x		x	
William F. Quinn president, Dole Co. (food)	x	x		
M. J. Rathbone former chairman, Standard Oil of New Jersey				
Samuel Reber foreign service officer				
Roland L. Redmond lawyer, Carter, Ledyard & Milburn				
Philip D. Reed former chairman, General Electric	x			
William G. Reed chairman, Simpson Timber Co.		x		
Whitelaw Reid former chairman, New York *Herald Tribune*				
G. Frederick Reinhardt senior director, Stanford Research Institute International	x			
Stanley R. Resor lawyer, Debevoise, Plimpton, Lyons & Gates				
James B. Reston vice president, *New York Times*				
Lloyd G. Reynolds economist, Yale University				
Richard S. Rheem former president, Rheem Manufacturing Co.	x	x	x	
Alfred Rheinstein president, Rheinstein Construction Co.				
Philip H. Rhinelander philosopher, Stanford University	x			

LI	CE	CFR	CED	BC	
					Governor of Hawaii, 1957-62
			x	x	
	x	x			
x	x				
x		x	x	x	
x					
	x	x			
		x			Foreign Service Officer, 1937-68
x		x			Sec'y of Army, 1965-69
	x	x			
	x	x			
x					
	x	x			
	x				

APPENDIX OF HEAVIES

Name and Occupation

Name and Occupation	BO	PU	CA	RA
Edward V. Rickenbacker former chairman, Eastern Airlines	x			
Torkild Rieber former chairman, The Texas Co. (oil)	x			
S. Dillon Ripley II zoologist; secretary, Smithsonian Institution				
Geroid T. Robinson historian, Columbia University				
James M. Roche chairman, General Motors				
David Rockefeller chairman, Chase Manhattan Bank				
John D. Rockefeller III chairman, Rockefeller Foundation				
Nelson A. Rockefeller former chairman, Rockefeller Center				
Alvin J. Rockwell lawyer, Brobeck, Phleger & Harrison	x	x		
Karl B. Rodi lawyer, Wellborn, Barrett & Rodi			x	x
James G. Rogers lawyer; educator				
Lindsay Rogers public law professor, Columbia University				
Haakon I. Romnes chairman, AT & T				
Robert V. Roosa investment banker, Brown Brothers Harriman & Co.				
Oren Root director, Irving Trust Co.				

Major Government Positions

LI	CE	CFR	CED	BC	
x					
x					
	x	x			
	x	x			
		x		x	Member, National Commission on Productivity, 1969
x	x	x		x	Member, Task Force on International Development, 1969
	x	x			Chairman, Commission on Population Growth and the American Future, 1969-71
	x	x			Asst. Sec'y of State, 1944-45; Special Asst. to the President, 1954-55; Governor of New York, 1958-
					Special Asst. to U.S. Attorney General, 1940-43; General Counsel, N.L.R.B., 1944-45
	x	x			Asst. Sec'y of State, 1931-33
	x	x			Consultant, Senate Foreign Relations Committee, 1965
			x	x	
	x	x			Economist, Federal Reserve Bank of New York, 1946-60; Under Sec'y of Treasury, 1961-64
x	x	x			

APPENDIX OF HEAVIES

Name and Occupation	In-Group Connection			
	BO	PU	CA	RA
Axel G. Rosin president, Book-of-the-Month-Club, Inc.				
Thomas J. Ross chairman, T. J. Ross & Associates (public relations)		x		
Eugene V. Rostow former dean; law professor, Yale University				
William M. Roth former chairman, Pacific National Life Assurance	x	x		
Albert B. Ruddock director, Security First National Bank	x		x	
Chester A. Rude former vice chairman, Security First National Bank			x	x
Oscar M. Ruebhausen director, International Basic Economy Corp.				
James A. Runser accountant, Haskins & Sells	x	x		
Dean Rusk former president, Rockefeller Foundation				
Donald J. Russell chairman, Southern Pacific	x	x	x	
George Russell vice chairman, General Motors				
Harrison Ryon lawyer, Schauer, Ryon & McIntyre			x	x
Harrison E. Salisbury assistant managing editor, *New York Times*				
Charles E. Saltzman investment banker, Goldman, Sachs & Co.				
Howland H. Sargeant president, Radio Liberty Committee, Inc.				

Major Government Positions

LI	CE	CFR	CED	BC	
	x	x	x		
		x			
	x	x			Under Sec'y of State, 1966-69
		x	x		Special Trade Negotiator, 1963-69
	x	x			
	x	x			Sec'y of State, 1961-69
x				x	
x			x		
	x	x			
	x	x			Under Sec'y of State, 1954-55
	x	x			Officer, State Dept., 1947-53

219

APPENDIX OF HEAVIES

| Name and Occupation | \multicolumn{4}{c}{In-Group Connection} |

Name and Occupation	BO	PU	CA	RA
Stuart T. Saunders former chairman, Penn Central				
John E. Sawyer president, Williams College				
Arthur M. Schlesinger, Jr. historian, City University of New York				
Adolph W. Schmidt vice president, Thomas Mellon & Sons				
Benno C. Schmidt partner, John Hay Whitney & Co. (investments)		x	x	
Edward J. Schneider vice president, Crocker-Citizens National Bank	x	x		
Frederick A. O. Schwarz lawyer, Davis, Polk, Wardwell, Sunderland & Kiendl				
Stuart N. Scott lawyer, Dewey, Ballantine, Bushby, Palmer & Wood				
William P. Scott, Jr. owner, Scott Co. (heating)	x	x	x	
Glenn T. Seaborg chemist; former chancellor, U. of California, Berkeley	x			
Ralph W. Seely vice president, U.S. Steel		x	x	
Frederick Seitz president, Rockefeller University	x			
Robert B. Semple president, Wyandotte Chemicals Corp.	x			
Porter Sesnon partner, Porter Estate Co. (investments)	x	x		x
Porter Sesnon, Jr. partner, Porter Estate Co.	x	x		

Major Government Positions

LI	CE	CFR	CED	BC	
x				x	
	x	x			
	x	x			Special Asst. to the President, 1961-64
x	x	x			Ambassador to Canada, 1969-
x					Economics Division, State Dept., 1945-46
x	x	x			
	x	x			
		x			Chairman, A.E.C., 1961-
	x				Science Adviser, NATO, 1959-60; Chairman, Defense Science Board, 1964-68
x			x		

Name and Occupation	In-Group Connection			
	BO	PU	CA	RA
William T. Sesnon rancher; oil producer	x	x	x	
Whitney N. Seymour lawyer, Simpson, Thatcher & Bartlett				
James G. Shea public relations manager, Southern Pacific	x		x	
Frederick Sheffield lawyer, Webster, Sheffield, Fleischmann, Hitchcock & Chrystie				
David Shepard former executive vice president, Standard Oil of New Jersey				
Frank P. Shepard former vice president, Bankers Trust Co.				
James G. Shields, Jr. chairman, California Canadian Bank	x	x	x	
William L. Shirer author; journalist				
J. Robert Shuman partner, Shuman, Agnew & Co. (stock brokers)	x	x		
John R. Shuman partner, Shuman, Agnew & Co.	x	x		
Forrest N. Shumway president, Signal Oil & Gas	x		x	
Roy Shurtleff investment banker, Blyth & Co.	x	x		
George N. Shuster former president, Hunter College				
Shermer L. Sibley president, Pacific Gas & Electric	x	x		

LI	CE	CFR	CED	BC	Major Government Positions
	x	x			
	x	x			
	x	x			
	x	x			
	x	x			
	x	x			Advisor, State Dept., 1944–45
				x	

APPENDIX OF HEAVIES

Name and Occupation	In-Group Connection			
	BO	PU	CA	RA
John L. Simpson consultant, Bechtel Construction Corp.	x	x		
Ellis D. Slater former chairman, Emery Air Freight Corp.				
Joseph E. Slater president, Salk Institute				
John J. Slocum division chief, Federal Deposit Insurance Corporation				
Willis S. Slusser general counsel, Bechtel Construction Corp.	x	x		
Carlton S. Smith musicologist, New York University				
Cyrus R. Smith former chairman, American Airlines	x			
David P. Smith investment banker, Scudder, Stevens & Clark	x	x		
David S. Smith lawyer, Baker, McKenzie & Hightower				
Ritchie C. Smith officer, City Transfer Storage Co.	x	x		
Russell G. Smith advisory board member, Bank of America	x	x		
W. Mason Smith lawyer, Root, Barrett, Cohen, Knapp & Smith				
Peter C. A. Solbert lawyer, Davis, Polk, Wardwell, Sunderland & Kiendl				
Emmett G. Solomon president, Crocker-Citizens National Bank	x	x	x	
Charles H. Sommer, Jr. chairman, Monsanto Chemical Co.				

LI	CE	CFR	CED	BC	
	x	x			
x			x		
	x	x			Deputy Asst. Sec'y of State, 1960-61
	x	x			
	x	x			
x				x	Sec'y of Commerce, 1968-69
x		x			Asst. Sec'y of Air Force, 1954-59
	x	x			
	x	x			Deputy Asst. Sec'y of Defense, 1963-65
x					
x				x	

APPENDIX OF HEAVIES

Name and Occupation	In-Group Connections			
	BO	PU	CA	RA
Davidson Sommers general counsel, Equitable Life Assurance Society				
H. Christian Sonne chairman, National Planning Association				
Carl B. Spaeth former dean, Stanford Law School	x			
Monroe E. Spaght chairman, Shell Oil Co.		x		
Joseph P. Spang, Jr. former chairman, Gillette Co.				
Percy C. Spencer former chairman, Sinclair Oil Co.				
William M. Spencer director, North American Car Corp.	x			x
Charles M. Spofford lawyer, Davis, Polk, Wardwell, Sunderland & Kiendl				
Robert C. Sprague chairman, Sprague Electric Co.				
Allan Sproul former president, Federal Reserve Bank of New York	x			
Frank Stanton president, C.B.S.				
Harold Stassen lawyer, Stassen, Kephart, Sarkiis & Scullin				
Hans Stauffer director, Stauffer Chemical Co.	x			
Edward L. Steiniger president, Sinclair Oil Co.				
Claude O. Stephens chairman, Texas Gulf Sulphur				

226

LI	CE	CFR	CED	BC	
	x	x			Special Asst. to Sec'y of War, 1946; General Counsel, World Bank, 1949-59
		x	x		
		x			Special Asst. to Asst. Sec'y of State, 1945-46
x					
x			x		
x		x			
x	x	x			
		x	x		Consultant, National Security Council, 1954-58
	x		x		
	x	x	x	x	
	x	x			Governor of Minnesota, 1938-45; Special Asst. to the President, 1955-58
x					
x		x			
x		x			

227

APPENDIX OF HEAVIES

Name and Occupation	In-Group Connections			
	BO	PU	CA	RA
J. E. Wallace Sterling chancellor, Stanford University	x		x	
John P. Stevens, Jr. director, J. P. Stevens & Co. (textiles)				
Robert T. Stevens chairman, J. P. Stevens & Co.				
Roger L. Stevens real estate investor; theatrical producer	x			
Samuel S. Stevens lawyer, Heller, Ehrman, White & McAuliffe	x	x	x	
John R. Stevenson lawyer, Sullivan & Cromwell				
Ron Stever president, Stever & Co. (pension consultants)	x		x	
Arthur C. Stewart former senior vice president, Union Oil Co.		x	x	
Potter Stewart associate justice, United States Supreme Court	x			
Samuel B. Stewart executive vice president, Bank of America	x	x		
William L. Stewart former chairman, Union Oil Co.	x	x	x	
Chauncey Stillman chairman, Homeland Foundation				
Ralph S. Stillman executive committee chairman, Marine Midland Grace Trust				
George D. Stoddard former chancellor, New York University				

LI	CE	CFR	CED	BC	
	x*	x			
x			x		
x				x	Sec'y of Army, 1953-55
	x				Special Asst. to the President on Arts, 1964- ; Chairman, National Endowment for the Arts, 1965-
x		x			Legal Adviser, State Dept., 1969-
	x				
	x	x			Special Adviser, Defense Dept., 1947; Member, National Security Council Staff, 1948-51
x		x			
	x	x			

229

Name and Occupation	In-Group Connection			
	BO	PU	CA	RA
Isaac N. Stokes lawyer, Webster, Sheffield, Fleischmann, Hitchcock & Chrystie				
William C. Stolk former chairman, American Can Co.		x		
Shepard Stone director for international affairs, Ford Foundation				
Thomas M. Storke former publisher, Santa Barbara *News-Press*			x	x
Dorsey E. Straitliff president, Rocky Mountain Drilling Co.	x		x	
Julius A. Stratton chairman of the board, Ford Foundation				
Donald B. Straus president, American Arbitration Association				
Lewis L. Strauss former investment banker, Kuhn, Loeb & Co.				
Benjamin Strong former president, Chase Manhattan Bank				
Mark R. Sullivan former chairman, Pacific Telephone & Telegraph		x	x	
Walter H. Sullivan, Jr. partner, Walter H. Sullivan & Sons (real estate)	x	x	x	
Eric Sutcliffe lawyer, Orrick, Dahlquist, Rowley & Sutcliffe	x	x		
Leif J. Sverdrup chairman, Sverdrup & Parcel (engineering consultants		x		
Lloyd Swayne vice president, San Francisco Warehouse Co.	x	x		

LI	CE	CFR	CED	BC	
	x	x			
x			x		
	x	x			
					U.S. Senator from California, 1938-39
	x	x			
	x	x			
	x	x		x	Chairman, A.E.C., 1953-58; Sec'y of Commerce, 1958-59
x	x	x			
x					
x					

APPENDIX OF HEAVIES

Name and Occupation	In-Group Connection			
	BO	PU	CA	RA
Lloyd Swayne, Jr. president, San Francisco Warehouse Co.	x	x		
William A. Swinerton president, Swinerton & Walberg (builders)		x	x	
Jacquelin A. Swords lawyer, Cadwalader, Wickersham & Taft				
Henry Gardiner Symonds chairman, Tenneco	x	x		
Nathaniel M. Symonds senior vice president, Northern Trust Co.	x		x	
Phillips Talbot political scientist				
A. Thomas Taylor chairman, Deltec International				
Waller Taylor II lawyer, Adams, Duque & Hazeltine	x		x	
Walter N. Thayer president, Whitney Communications Corp.				
Wellman P. Thayer lawyer, Thayer & Copes			x	x
Alfred R. Thomas investment banker, Dean Witter & Co.	x		x	
Charles A. Thomas chairman, Monsanto Chemical Co.				
Charles S. Thomas former president, Trans World Airlines			x	
Evan Thomas vice president, W. W. Norton				
Joseph A. Thomas investment banker, Lehman Brothers		x		

Major Government Positions

LI	CE	CFR	CED	BC	
x	x				
x			x		
	x	x			Asst. Sec'y of State, 1961-65; Ambassador to Greece, 1965-68
x				x	
x					
x			x		
x				x	Consultant, National Security Council, 1953
x					Sec'y of Navy, 1954-57
	x	x			
x					

APPENDIX OF HEAVIES

Name and Occupation	In-Group Connection			
	BO	PU	CA	RA
Earle S. Thompson chairman, Alleghany Power System, Inc.				
Kenneth W. Thompson vice president, Rockefeller Foundation				
Charles B. Thornton chairman, Litton Industries			x	
Willard L. Thorp economist, Amherst College				
Cyril R. Tobin senior partner, Tobin & Tobin	x	x		
John C. Traphagen former chairman, Bank of New York				
William J. Travers executive vice president, Atlantic Richfield		x	x	
Juan T. Trippe former chairman, Pan American World Airways				
David B. Truman president, Mount Holyoke College				
Jasper W. Tully former president, Reserve Oil Co.		x	x	
H. C. Turner, Jr. chairman, Turner Construction Co.			x	
Edward R. Valentine president, Robinson Building Co.			x	
Arthur B. Van Buskirk vice president, Thomas Mellon & Sons				
Cyrus R. Vance lawyer, Simpson, Thacher & Bartlett				
Henry P. Van Dusen former president, Union Theological Seminary				

LI	CE	CFR	CED	BC	
	x	x			
	x	x			
			x	x	
	x	x			Asst. Sec'y of State, 1946-52
x	x	x			
x		x		x	
	x	x			
x			x		
x					
x			x		
x	x	x			Sec'y of Navy, 1962-63; Deputy Sec'y of Defense, 1964-67
	x	x			

235

APPENDIX OF HEAVIES

Name and Occupation	In-Group Connection			
	BO	PU	CA	RA
Guido F. Verbeck, Jr. senior vice president, Morgan Guaranty Trust	x			
Howard G. Vesper vice president, Chevron Oil Co.	x	x	x	
John C. Virden chairman, Goodyear Tire & Rubber				
Harry J. Volk president, Union Bank of Los Angeles	x		x	
Daniel G. Volkmann, Jr. architect, Bull, Field, Volkmann & Stockwell	x	x		
Richard Walberg chairman, Swinerton & Walberg (builders)	x	x	x	
A. Lightfoot Walker president, Rheem Manufacturing Co.		x		
Frank F. Walker investment banker, Dean Witter & Co.	x	x		
George G. Walker chairman, Electric Bond & Share Co.				
Robert W. Walker vice president, Atchison, Topeka & Santa Fe Railway	x		x	
Robert E. Wallace vice president, Federal Insurance Co.	x	x	x	
Kenneth Walsh manager, Best Way System Draying Co.	x	x		
Frederick M. Warburg investment banker, Kuhn, Loeb & Co.				
F. Champion Ward vice president, Ford Foundation				
Rawleigh Warner, Jr. president, Mobil Oil Co.				

LI	CE	CFR	CED	BC
x				
x				x
		x		
	x	x		
	x	x		
	x	x		
x		x		x

APPENDIX OF HEAVIES

Name and Occupation	In-Group Connections			
	BO	PU	CA	RA
Robert S. Warner accountant, Lybrand, Ross	x		x	
John E. Warren president, Cities Service Co.				
Lingan A. Warren former president, Safeway Stores		x		
William C. Warren dean, Columbia University Law School				
Edward H. Wasson president, Pacific Telephone & Telegraph	x		x	
R. Gordon Wasson former vice president, Morgan Guaranty Trust				
Thomas J. Watson, Jr. chairman, IBM				
Paul L. Wattis president, Lakeview Mining Co.	x	x		
Bethuel M. Webster lawyer, Webster, Sheffield, Fleischmann, Hitchcock & Chrystie				
Leo D. Welch former executive vice president, Standard Oil of New Jersey				
Herman B. Wells chancellor, Indiana University				
George S. Wheaton executive vice president, Dillingham Corp.	x	x	x	
W. H. Wheeler chairman, Pitney-Bowes, Inc.				
Gilbert F. White geographer, University of Colorado				
John R. White accountant, Price, Waterhouse & Co.	x		x	

LI	CE	CFR	CED	BC	
x		x			
x					
x	x				Consultant, Treasury Dept., 1947-49
	x	x			
x		x		x	
	x	x			Asst. to Attorney General, 1927-29
x		x			
	x	x			
		x	x	x	
	x	x			

APPENDIX OF HEAVIES

Name and Occupation	In-Group Connections			
	BO	PU	CA	RA
Theodore H. White author; journalist				
William Whiteford lawyer, Whiteford, Taylor & Preston	x			
Dwight Whiting vice president, Alexander & Alexander (insurance)	x		x	
George N. Whiting partner, El Toro Co.	x		x	
Frederick B. Whitman president, Western Pacific Railroad	x	x		
John Hay Whitney partner, John Hay Whitney & Co. (investments)				
Arnold Whitridge president, New York Society Library				
Leland K. Whittier chairman, M. H. Whittier Co.	x	x	x	
Myron A. Wick, Jr. investment banker, Dominick & Dominick		x		
Brayton Wilbur, Jr. vice president, Wilbur, Ellis Co. (exports)	x	x		
Frazar B. Wilde former chairman, Connecticut General Life Insurance				
Walter W. Wilds vice president, Gulf Oil Corp.				
Langbourne M. Williams chairman, Freeport Sulphur Co.				
Joseph H. Willitts economist, University of Pennsylvania				
Lucius Wilmerding, Jr. political economist				

LI	CE	CFR	CED	BC	
	x	x			
x					
x					
x	x	x		x	Ambassador to Great Britain, 1956-61
	x	x			
x					
x		x	x		
x		x			
	x	x		x	
	x	x			
	x	x			

APPENDIX OF HEAVIES

Name and Occupation	BO	PU	CA	RA
Carroll L. Wilson former president, Metals & Controls Corp.				
Charles E. Wilson former chairman, General Electric				
Donald M. Wilson vice president, Time, Inc.				
Walter W. Wilson investment banker, Morgan Stanley & Co.				
Henry S. Wingate chairman, International Nickel Co.				
David J. Winton chairman, Kenwood Oil Co.				
Dean Witter, Jr. investment banker, Dean Witter & Co.	x	x		
Jean C. Witter investment banker, Dean Witter & Co.	x	x		
Thomas W. Witter investment banker, Dean Witter & Co.	x	x		
Wendell W. Witter investment banker, Dean Witter & Co.	x	x		
William D. Witter president, Wm. D. Witter, Inc.	x	x		
William M. Witter investment banker, Dean Witter & Co.	x	x		
Thomas Wolfe president, Wolfe Property Co.			x	x
Bryce Wood political scientist				
Robert W. Woodruff former chairman, Coca-Cola				

In-Group Connections

LI	CE	CFR	CED	BC	
	x	x			
x			x	x	
	x	x			
x			x		
		x		x	
	x	x			Deputy Asst. Sec'y of Army, 1948
x					
x					
x					
	x	x			
x				x	

APPENDIX OF HEAVIES

Name and Occupation	In-Group Connection			
	BO	PU	CA	RA
Leslie B. Worthington former president, U.S. Steel		x		
Fulton W. Wright vice president, Matson Navigation Co.	x		x	
Henry M. Wriston former president, Brown University; Council on Foreign Relations; The American Assembly				
Walter B. Wriston chairman, First National City Bank of New York				
Charles E. Wyzanski, Jr. former lawyer, Ropes & Gray				
Adam Yarmolinsky law professor, Harvard University				
J. Perry Yates executive vice president, Bechtel Construction Corp.		x	x	
Theodore Yntema former vice president, Ford Motor Co.				
Charles W. Yost foreign service officer				
Kenneth T. Young president, Asia Society				
Carl U. Zachrisson political scientist, Pitzer College	x			x
Arnold J. Zurcher vice president, Alfred P. Sloan Foundation				

LI	CE	CFR	CED	BC	
x					
	x	x			
x		x			
	x	x			Solicitor, Labor Dept., 1933-35; Special Asst. to U.S. Attorney General, 1935-37
	x	x			Special Asst. to Sec'y of Defense, 1961-64; Deputy Asst. Sec'y of Defense, 1965-66
		x	x		
	x	x			Ambassador to the UN, 1969-71
	x	x			Ambassador to Thailand, 1961-63
	x	x			

Index

(A complete listing of club members will be found in the Appendix.)

247

74 75 76 77 10 9 8 7 6 5 4 3 2 1